THE
Bonsai
IDENTIFIER

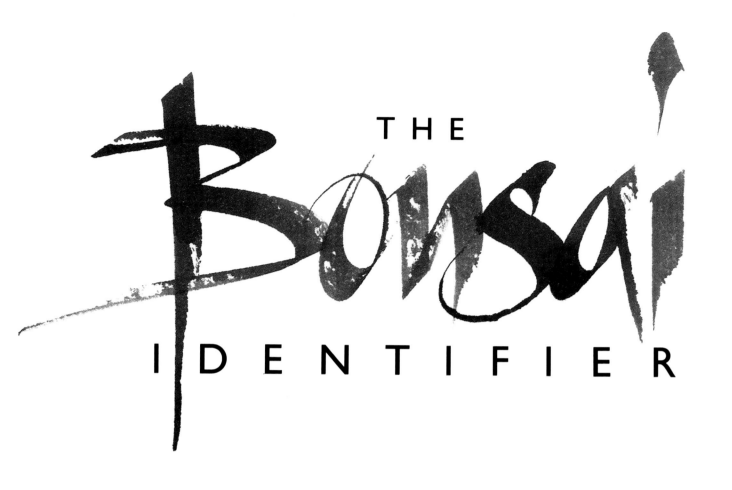

THE Bonsai IDENTIFIER

GORDON OWEN

NEW
BURLINGTON
BOOKS

A QUINTET BOOK

Published by New Burlington Books
6 Blundell Street
London, N7 9BH

ISBN 1-85348-281-1

Reprinted 1995

This book was designed and produced by
Quintet Publishing Limited
6 Blundell Street
London N7 9BH

Creative Director: Peter Bridgewater
Art Director: Ian Hunt
Designer: Louise Morley
Artwork: Danny McBride
Project Editor: Judith Simons
Editor: Carol Hupping Fisher
Illustrator: Lorraine Harrison

Typeset in Great Britain by
Central Southern Typesetters, Eastbourne
Manufactured in Hong Kong by
Regent Publishing Services Limited
Printed in China by
Leefung-Asco Printers Limited

CONTENTS

INTRODUCTION

Bonsai is often referred to as the Japanese art of miniature trees. Its origins, however, are in China. The word bonsai comes from the Chinese words *pun sai.* It was the Chinese who developed many of the creation and training techniques and then exported them to Japan over 500 years ago. The Japanese mastered the techniques involved and introduced them to the Western world, where the creation of bonsai is now an ever-growing hobby, if the unintentional pun can be excused.

In biblical days trees and shrubs were grown in pots to make them transportable and probably to allow ready access to leaves and bark for use in medicinal preparations. Growing a tree in a pot solely for enjoyment

was a logical progression, and the development of training happened gradually as people saw ways in which they could make minor improvements to what Nature had already created.

Originally trees for bonsai were collected from the wild, and usually from quite inaccessible and dangerous places high up in the mountains and from the faces of sheer cliffs. Much skill and nerve were needed, and precise rituals were followed prior to collection. At one time collecting the creations of Nature from the wild was a recognized profession in Japan. In the collecting areas there were even nurseries set up for the specific purpose of acclimatizing trees before bringing them down to the plains and putting

RIGHT A selection of small-scale *(mame)* bonsai of Chinese origin.

them in decorative pots. Those collected plants were, and still are, more highly prized as bonsai than those created by people.

Nowadays in Japan, and in most other countries, collecting bonsai from the wild is usually prohibited unless a special permit has been granted. Most of today's bonsai are not found, but created with human skill, starting from seed, cuttings, layers or grafts. In Japan the art of bonsai has become a sizeable industry that includes the growing of quality starter material and partially trained trees, both for export and for further development by the Japanese bonsai trade. Superior quality and older material goes to the top-class bonsai nurseries for development into bonsai masterpieces.

THE MEANING OF 'BONSAI'

A bonsai consists of two elements: the living plant and the container. The plant may be a vine, a shrub or a tree, but is colloquially referred to as simply a tree. The container is usually a conventional pot or a slab of flat but interesting rock. Or the plant may even be growing on a rock with the roots buried in pockets of soil. A bonsai should not be referred to as a bonsai tree. The word already includes the living element. Also once out of a pot a tree ceases to be a bonsai.

The word bonsai should be pronounced with the accent on 'sai', as in 'sighing'. It is Japanese and when translated means a planting in a tray. But a bonsai is something more than just a planting in a tray. The two elements have to be in harmony and the selection of the right pot for a tree is almost an art in itself.

To understand that a bonsai is not just any miniature tree, growing in any container, one should see top-quality bonsai in Japan. There, trees several hundred years old are found growing in containers. They are truly living works of art, having been carefully attended to over the years and handed down

ABOVE *Juniperus communis* 'Hornbrookii, a dwarf cultivar of Common juniper, informally styled with a sinuous trunk; height 35 cm (14 in); age 15 years.

RIGHT Growing benches of partially trained bonsai in the grounds of a private collection in Japan.

BELOW *Murraya paniculata* – commonly known as Satinwood, Orange jasmine or the Cosmetic bark tree: height 115 cm (45 in); age 100 years. This species is grown out of doors in the East but is an indoor subject in the West.

OPPOSITE *Pyracantha angustifolia*: height 56 cm (22 in); age approximately 70 years.

from father to son. Most bonsai encountered in the West will only be shadows of what a bonsai should be in form and spirit.

Age is a factor in bonsai, but it is not important in itself. Being old does not necessarily mean that it is a better bonsai than one that is much younger. What is important are the characteristics of age. While people can do much to enhance the illusion of age, true age is accompanied by the formation of mature bark, solid trunks and buttressing roots. In certain species the bark may be deeply furrowed and raised as much as 5 cm (2 in) in really old specimens. This quality of bark only forms with the passage of time, and its

production cannot be rushed; however, growing the bonsai in the open ground for a number of years helps considerably.

OUTDOOR AND INDOOR BONSAI

Many people are surprised to learn that most bonsai spend all of their time outdoors. They may think that bonsai are delicate and need the protection of an indoor environment. This is possibly because when they see bonsai on display they are usually in an indoor setting, either in a store or at a flower show. Some trees may indeed be overwintered indoors in an unheated room or greenhouse, but many will be left outdoors all the time, perhaps with an occasional watering so that they do not dry out.

Some species do need to be moved indoors or sheltered outside during particularly cold weather. A bonsai is generally not as hardy as the same species growing in the ground. This is because when growing naturally, the plant's roots descend a considerable way into the earth, and unless frost penetrates particularly deeply, the roots do not usually get touched by it. But in a small amount of soil roots are more vulnerable to frost and need to be protected.

There are, of course, species that make what are called indoor bonsai, and there is a considerable demand for such bonsai at the present time. Despite their popularity they can be difficult to maintain, and many trees are lost through a lack of understanding of their general horticultural needs. Many indoor bonsai are treated as house plants, and fed and watered like house plants when they really should be treated like trees. The species used for indoor bonsai are usually subtropical or tropical plants, and while they like being outdoors in the summer, they need to be kept well above freezing for all of the year. Some demand high room temperatures both during the day and the night, making them difficult to care for.

A LIVING ART FORM

For many years bonsai has been recognized as an art form in Japan. Unfortunately in the West such recognition is still far away, due partially to the lack of bonsai tradition here and the need for new caretakers to maintain and develop the trees further after their previous owners die.

Bonsai is a living art form. Once set, the shape needs to be maintained, and the design changed now and again, as one part develops more than another, or as the grower sees the tree in a different light from time to time. The design is never really finished, as there is usually some subtle improvement that can be made. The new growth provides an ever-moving canvas upon which to 'paint' the bonsai unceasingly.

SHAPES AND STYLES

Look at a few trees growing naturally and you will see an infinite variety of shapes. Move to another environment and different shapes will be found for the very same species. Trees may be found growing singly, in small groups, or in large forests. Some may have one or more trunks, and sometimes trees that have been blown down have trunks that have rooted themselves so that the remaining branches form a line of new stems. Some trees will be slightly sloping; others will have taken on a definite windswept look, as though high on a hill or near the coast, battling against the prevailing winds. Roots may even be exposed and growing over solid rock, covering the sides of it in sheets, or even grasping the rock like the tentacles of an octopus. Other trees may have lost their apex because they were struck by lightning, or their trunks were bared of bark and sanded smooth by particles of wind-blown sand.

Bonsai will be found that reflect all these natural shapes and arrangements, and to each bonsai can be ascribed a particular

BELOW Scots pines *(Pinus sylvestris)* created in the literati style from six-year-old specimens grown from seed.

style. The number of variations on the basic styles is almost endless. The basic styles of bonsai are taken from the slant of the trunk, which can go from the pure vertical, to almost perpendicular in the formal cascade, through multiple trunks, to group plantings of one or more trees, right to massive plantings that may take several men to move. Rarely will you see four or six trees presented together because such numbers are difficult to arrange successfully.

There are also styles associated with rocks, and even roots that will be exposed from time to time, giving the feeling that through alluvial action the soil has been washed away.

The Literati Style

In Japan the bonsai production industry concentrates on species that can be propagated easily and made into reasonable bonsai in less than 10 years, and in those styles that are marketable or can be readily transported. For this reason many quite common species, and some styles such as cascades, are not produced commercially; thus it is rare to see cascade bonsai other than what is individually produced.

Styles of tree and species come in and out of fashion, and individual conceptions of what bonsai should look like dictate the styles in which individuals create them. Many who grow what they believe to be bonsai are

simply happy to keep alive a piece of material that would otherwise make a tree of major size, no matter what it looks like. Others understand what makes a true bonsai and strive to produce trees that measure up to that concept; they realize that bonsai take many years to come of age. There are no genuine shortcuts, despite the enhancements that can be made which add to the illusion of age.

All these styles have rules or guidelines associated with them, but there is one style that is completely free-form and without any formal rules – the literati style. This is a style that is used for thin-trunked trees that have little foliage so that nothing detracts from the interesting changes in their trunks or branch lines. Because this style has no specific rules, the result can be very variable, and it is a style that is far more difficult to create successfully than any other.

SIZE

A bonsai can vary in height from a few centimetres (1 in) to a metre or so (several feet). The average height of a bonsai in the West is probably around 46 cm (18 in). The definition of a bonsai prescribes no size limits, although it is generally accepted that a bonsai has to be compact, artistic and a miniature representation of a tree growing in Nature. When heights are mentioned in books the measurement is usually of the height of the tree itself rather than the bonsai as a whole. Sometimes the spread is also given.

Whatever the size, be it 1.5 m (5 ft) for the atrium of a corporate headquarters foyer or just 15 cm (6 in) high so that you can hold it in the palm of your hand, the trunk must exhibit stature and power, with taper and with flaring roots. The surface must look as though the tree has been living in the same small pot of soil all its life. Too little attention is yet paid to these important aspects in the West, where many trees in pots are only of sapling status.

For the vast majority of bonsai, the ratio of the trunk diameter at ground level to the height of the tree should be around six to one, except when the tree is clearly meant to have a thin trunk. Very few trees in the West will measure up to this standard, so when you see one that does, you may well be looking at a tree truly worthy of being called a bonsai, rather than just an interesting piece of greenery in a container.

BONSAI MATERIAL

The range of material used for bonsai is almost limitless, but is confined to plants that have woody stems, whether they be trees, shrubs or vines. Many genera of tree are widespread throughout the Northern Hemisphere, so from one country to another similar species will be seen. Those trees common locally are also likely to feature more heavily than exotics, and the number of species that could be made into bonsai is almost endless.

The materials used for bonsai are normal plants growing in miniature with their roots contained in a confined space; they have the potential to make a tree of full size if returned to the ground. It may well take a number of years before re-establishing themselves and commencing to make rampant growth. Bonsai are not made from genetic dwarfs,

ABOVE Japanese white pine *(Pinus parviflora)* showing exposed roots.

LEFT Japanese mountain maple *(Acer palmatum)*: height 60 cm (24 in); age 25 years. The bonsai is shown just coming into leaf.

ABOVE A display of small-scale bonsai in the gardens of a Japanese private collection.

TOP Japanese mountain maple *(Acer palmatum):* height 98 cm (39 in); age 90 years.

and the use of such material is frowned upon by some. Others argue that it is acceptable to keep a dwarf species as a bonsai if it is less than one-sixth of its normal height. How important this is, is debatable, but the favoured juniper variety in Japan, Shimpakie juniper (*Juniperus chinensis sargentii*) is often seen at its maximum height when in a bonsai pot!

SEASONAL DISPLAYS

All species have their best seasons, whether it be in the winter when out of leaf, early spring, summer or autumn. The changes that spring heralds can truly excite the spirit, as Larch break into new growth or some of the ornamental Maples display fiery reds after a drab winter. In late spring and summer come showy displays of Crab apple blossoms and many other delightful sights, such as Wisteria and Laburnum displaying long racemes of mauve or yellow flowers. Many species show a range of magnificent colours in their leaves in autumn, or have ripe and colourful fruits presenting a burst of late colour before winter sets in. Even when all foliage has dropped, stems and buds can be beautiful in their fine tracery, and long-lasting fruit may still be hanging on the tree.

A bonsai should only be displayed when in perfect health and at the peak of condition. For many trees this period is quite limited, while for others, like Pine and Juniper bonsai, it can extend to almost the whole of the year.

In both China and Japan many deciduous trees are only shown in their winter clothes, and it is not uncommon for them to be completely defoliated before show time so that they can be displayed out of leaf. When trees are shown out of leaf they have to be of an exceptional quality, as any blemishes and design faults will be visible, no longer being masked by foliage.

The vast majority of bonsai that are likely to be seen in the West will have one best view – the front – and will usually have been developed with distinct back and front sides. The Chinese concept is to have trees that can be viewed from both the back and the front, but their idea of bonsai at present is quite different to what we know in the West, which is more readily identified with Japanese bonsai. We in the West prefer trunks to taper and branches to be more fully clothed. We prefer to display trees not leaning back but slightly forwards, and if two or more trees are grouped together, they are not planted in a straight row across the centre line of the container.

VIEWING POSITION

Whatever the concept of a particular bonsai, it needs to be viewed from its optimum position to be fully appreciated. That is from a distance of about twice the height of the tree and slightly looking down at the surface, but mainly up into the canopy, just as you would view a tree growing in open parkland. This is also the position from which it will have been viewed and studied when being developed into a bonsai by its grower. It is more often than not impossible to replicate this precise viewing position, so crouch down if necessary to enjoy a bonsai to its fullest.

PINCHING BACK, REPOTTING AND PRUNING

Confining the roots of a tree helps to keep the foliage in proportion, but constant pinching of the new growth is more important. This has to be done throughout the growing season to maintain the shape of the tree, otherwise it would quickly become an unstructured mess. Timing is important and is acquired with experience, but without pruning the tree will soon loose any artistic shape it has and skilful attention will be needed to reshape it.

Root-pruning is not done to keep a bonsai small: it is done to maintain and stimulate the vigour of the tree after it becomes potbound. Contrary to popular belief, bonsai do not need root-pruning each year. Some do, but with many, repotting every other year or even less frequently is all that is necessary. Really old Pines may only need to be repotted once every decade or even less frequently. Repotting tends to increase the growth rate of the tree and the size of the leaves, so is only undertaken if absolutely necessary. Some trees do not like being repotted and take a year or so to recover their normal vigour. Repotting is normally done just before the tree starts to make new growth in the spring, which could be early or late in the season, depending on the species and weather. Some flowering species are repotted in early autumn instead.

FLOWERING AND FRUITING

While foliage size can be reduced, flowers on bonsai remain the same size as flowers on normal-sized specimens, and if allowed to make fruit it, too, will reach full size unless removed earlier. Laburnum and Wisteria flowers, where they grow in the form of a long raceme, often do not reach the same length as when growing in the garden, but the individual elements of the flowers will be of full size. Bonsai go through the normal se-

quence of flowering and fruiting, just as they do when growing in the garden. The timings should in theory be the same, but much will depend on how the tree has been over-wintered. Cosseting the tree will bring on earlier leaf break and flowering.

WATERING AND FEEDING

It is far from the truth that to keep a bonsai small it has to be starved. To thrive it has to be fed regularly, and of course be kept watered. Bonsai are not house plants that have been especially bred to need little water, and pots can dry out very quickly, especially if there is a wind. Bonsai need as much water as they do in Nature, and as some species need more than others, some trees consequently need to be watered more frequently. The shape and depth of the pot also affects how much water is needed, because the greater the surface area in relation to the mass of compost, the quicker it will dry out.

Most bonsai will need watering at least once a day in the summer, and some twice a day, except in very wet weather. With heavy trunked trees that have massive flaring roots, most of the volume of the pot will be taken up, leaving only a comparatively small space for compost; in this case watering

ABOVE Dwarf Scots pine *(Pinus sylvestris 'Nana')*: height 50 cm (20 in); age over 20 years. This photograph shows the tree just a few weeks after basic shaping had been undertaken to create a new bonsai.

LEFT English or Field elm *(Ulmus procera)*: height 28cm (11 in); age 7 to 12 years. This specimen was started from cuttings and is here displayed on a slab of slate.

may be even more frequent than once or twice a day. The soil has to be free draining, and bonsai pots have drainage holes in the base to assist in this. The precise compost mix used much depends on the needs of the species and local growing conditions.

SHAPING TECHNIQUES

There are many techniques that can be used for shaping a bonsai. The most important of these is the use of either copper or aluminium wire. Wiring is needed now and again to maintain even a mature bonsai, and many a top-quality Pine will be found on display with much wire on it. If a tree is shown with wire on, the wire should be unobtrusive; none should be visible on the trunk. Many of the dead-wood effects seen on a bonsai will be man-made, and in some cases hours of carving with hand tools or mechanical aids will have taken place to enhance the illusion of age and to create fantastic artistic effects.

DISPLAYING BONSAI

When displayed bonsai are best enjoyed without the clutter of nearby objects. Ideally each should be on a stand of an appropriate size and design that is in harmony with the bonsai. Traditionally in Japan bonsai are brought indoors for a short time and placed in a *tokonoma* (alcove), where they are given pride of place. A tree appropriate to the season and occasion is chosen and dis-

played in association with an accent planting placed nearby. This is either of grasses, seasonal wild flowers growing in a decorative pot, a rock – a viewing stone – or a small bonsai; sometimes even a small incense burner is included in the arrangement. A scroll of some form is placed on the wall and again carefully chosen. All elements would be placed so as to be in harmony and for enjoyment as a cohesive whole, rather than as separate entities.

After being indoors for a few days the tree is then returned outside after first being re-acclimatized. In the winter this means placing the bonsai in a cold room for a day or so, particularly if it has been subjected to the drying effect of central heating. When the indoor humidity and temperature are substantially different from those outdoors, bonsai should only be brought indoors for a few days at a time.

POTS

The choice of pot is very important, for a tree can be made to look completely different when its pot is changed. The pot must be in sympathy with the species, and colours chosen in relation either to foliage, flowers or fruit – whichever is the most important. Glazed pots are usually used for deciduous species. Pines, Junipers and other conifers are often contained in dark, unglazed or only lightly glazed pots. Delicate-looking species need to be planted in pots that are light in appearance; heavy-looking ones are more suited to ponderous specimens like Black pines. All pots used for outdoor bonsai should be frost proof.

ARRANGING IN POTS

A tree is only placed centrally in a pot when the pot is round or square. At other times the tree will be placed slightly to one side and slightly behind lines drawn through the centre. This is for reasons of perspective and to give

a greater illusion of depth to the arrangement. Some deciduous species may be grown well to one side in very long, rectangular containers. This, together with suitable contouring of the surface, helps in the illusion of depth and space.

The surface of the compost itself should never be flat; if it is the tree will look as though it is sunken in the pot, and seem sad and shy. The tree should always be slightly raised up, and the base of the trunk should ideally be visible above the rim when viewed straight on. The tree should not be leaning backwards because it will seem as though it is falling away from you and look insecure and unstable. The apex of the tree will normally lean forward, as though the tree is bowing to its grower except when it is trained in the formal upright style.

GROUP PLANTINGS

Groups of trees should look natural, normally containing trees of differing size and stature. Only infrequently are different species mixed together. The overall silhouette should exhibit a triangular outline, just as should most other bonsai. Trees should not be evenly spaced or fill the pot fully. Some should be close together, others spaced apart a little, and all trunks should be visible from both the front and the side. There should be areas of open space. The ground should be contoured and covered with moss, and there should also be places where the eye is led into the group as though along a path. It should thus seem as though you could walk into the arrangement and explore its space. There are many variations on group plantings, and all have to be appreciated for what they are trying to express.

THE SPECIES DIRECTORY

There are many elements that contribute to a good bonsai, and pointers that can help one better appreciate a bonsai display can be found in the Species Directory that follows. In a book of this size it is not possible to discuss all of the numerous trees, shrubs and vines that could be or are used for bonsai. Rather, the Species Directory includes the main ones likely to be encountered either as home-produced trees or as imports. Some trees make more successful bonsai than others, and even in a given genus some species and varieties are better than others. This does not mean, however, that one should not experiment with less popular material from time to time, for by experimenting with unfamiliar plants much can sometimes be learned, and pleasant surprises can result.

BELOW *Mame* bonsai are displayed on a stand made especially for this purpose.

NOTES TO THE KEY

The members of certain genera can have species that are either shrubs or trees, and that may be either deciduous or evergreen. Some species are semi-evergreen, and depending on the climate of their habitat can be considered as either deciduous or evergreen, losing their leaves entirely only in severe winters.

All species have to flower and produce seed to perpetuate themselves, but when grown as a bonsai a species is denoted as flowering, fruiting or coning only where the flowers, fruit or cones are a significant feature.

There are over thirty recognized bonsai styles and many more possible variants. The categories used in the key are broad ones and have been selected to indicate the general level of variation in the styles possible, and those particularly appropriate to the genus.

Subjects shown as suitable for indoors may in some instances be grown outdoors depending on local conditions.

 Tree

 Evergreen

 Indoor

 Multitrunk styles

 Shrub

 Flowering

 Formal styles

 Literati style

 Vine

 Fruiting

 Informal styles

 Group plantings

 Deciduous

 Coning

 Cascading styles

 Mame size

ABIES SPP. FIR

DESCRIPTION

To many who have little knowledge of trees, every evergreen conifer is called a Fir. Surprisingly, most people will not have seen genuine Firs, as they are one of the least likely to be encountered as garden or countryside trees. They are easily distinguished from trees with similar foliage, like Yews and Hemlocks, by the two prominent white bands, called stomata, found on the back of the needlelike foliage. Firs are also characterized by shoots that are flattened with the needles in two ranks.

Firs make large trees. Their branch arrangement is in whorls, with a new one forming each year, and the bark is smooth but later forms blisters which carry resin. Only trees grown in isolation of others make good taper.

Firs are little used for bonsai in the West because suitable material is not readily available. Most of the species that are available in the West are unsuited to bonsai, having needles that are too long and stiff and thus difficult to work with to make a convincing specimen.

BONSAI STYLES AND PRESENTATION

Fir is best suited to formal and informal upright-style trees. Most of its branches, which are located towards the top of the trunk, should be at least horizontal but preferably raked down, whatever the style. Small groups and clumps are also very effective, either with or without the inclusion of some multistemmed trees in the arrangement. Long, thin-trunked specimens are likely to be seen in the literati style.

SPECIES AND VARIETIES

There are a number of species in this genus. The Japanese traditionally use Sakhalin fir (*A. sachalinensis*) and Japanese fir (*A. firma*).

The favoured species is usually Korean fir (*A. koreana*), as this is the main species of Fir likely to be found in garden centres. It makes a slow-growing small tree and is thus ideally suited to making into a bonsai, but some considerable expertise is needed to design a good specimen. It has bright green foliage and is a tree with much appeal, especially when it starts to produce its violet/purple cylindrical cones.

CARE

Some sun protection is needed during the height of summer, and frequent misting with water should be undertaken periodically. Its shape is maintained by pinching out the ends of new growth as it forms in the spring. Other than that it is a subject that demands little attention.

RIGHT Korean fir (*Abies koreana*) in the twin-tree style, showing its first cone at the apex; height 35 cm (14 in); age approximately 15 years.

ACER SPP. MAPLES

DESCRIPTION

Maples are one of the top three subjects used for bonsai, along with Pines and Junipers. They are seen very frequently, and many are produced commercially. Quality ranges from poor up to extremely good; the better-quality trees come from material that has grown in the open ground for a number of years.

Maples are a deciduous species of mainly small trees and shrubs that often come into leaf very early. They are distributed widely throughout the world, and many different species and varieties can be found. Apart from the general maple-leaf shape, there is considerable variety in leaf shape, quality and colour, and some are deeply incised. Their flowers are insignificant and easily over-looked. The fruit is in the form of a key, and only infrequently found on a Maple bonsai. Growth is usually upright or spreading.

BONSAI STYLES AND PRESENTATION

Bonsai Maples will be found growing in all conceivable forms, but usually in informal styles; they are frequently grown as small groups or forests, as well as growing with their roots over a rock. Better specimens will be planted in lightly glazed and quite shallow pots. The Japanese maples are grown for their early spring colour and for their autumn tints, which in some instances are particularly fiery and intense.

Maples shown in the West are usually in leaf, but in Japan they are more often displayed for the delicate ramification of branches and twigs that are most obvious outside of the growing season. If they are to be displayed in the middle of the growing season, they will often be defoliated first so that they can be shown out of leaf.

The finer-leaved Maples are grown with a

TOP Trident maple *(Acer buergeranum)*: height 57 cm (22 in); age unknown.

ABOVE *Acer palmatum* variety.

LEFT Japanese mountain
maple *(Acer palmatum):*
height 80 cm (31 in); age
80 years. The split trunk
adds to the illusion of age.

ABOVE *Acer palmatum
linearlobum,* a variety of
Japanese mountain maple:
height 50 cm (20 in);
age 10 years.

head of foliage less dense than the Trident maples (*A. buergeranum*). The latter are usually created with quite a dense head of foliage in which case the overall triangular silhouette is the important feature.

SPECIES AND VARIETIES

Field maples (*A. campestre*) are an excellent indigenous species, but most quality bonsai will be either Trident maples (*A. buergeranum*), or Japanese maples (*A. japonicum, A. palmatum*). The Japanese maples include the better spring and autumn coloured varieties such as Deshojo, Seigen, and the Dissectums. The latter have deeply cut and larger leaves that are light in appearance.

CARE

Maples are almost exclusively grown as outdoor bonsai. They need protection from winds, as leaf margins dry out quickly, spoiling their appearance. Midday sun should also be avoided. Winter protection is needed for the ornamental varieties. To keep leaves small, Maples are periodically defoliated in spring; a second flush of smaller leaves usually follows, and these go on to make better autumn colour. Maples should be repotted every two or three years.

BERBERIS SPP. BARBERRY

DESCRIPTION

Barberry is not a classical bonsai subject even though it is of oriental (and South American) origin. It is a shrub that has small leaves, thus making it ideal for bonsai. Some are deciduous and others evergreen, but the evergreens usually replace their leaves each year. Barberry flowers are small, daisylike and quite interesting, and go on to make interesting coloured fruit in the autumn. The flowers appear before the leaves open. Although they are not showy and can be overlooked, when viewed close up they have an unusual charm. Flowers are often red and orange in colour and come quite early in the year, when there is little activity or interest in most other species.

BONSAI STYLES AND PRESENTATION

A good time to enjoy a Barberry is when it is in flower. If the specimen is small, to appreciate it you need to approach closer to it than normal.

The best time for viewing, however, is when the leaves turn colour in the autumn and the tree is holding the bright red or dark blue-black fruits, depending upon the species. Barberries only make informal style bonsai, so the naturally erect and stiff-growing branches need to be softened by building curves through the stems and secondary branches. Particularly good-quality specimens are ones that have been dug up from the garden or the wild and have naturally acquired an interesting basal shape upon which a new head of foliage has developed.

Barberry groves are particularly effective when made with trees of different heights and sizes. The soil surface is contoured, and perhaps there are small rocks at strategically placed points. The inclusion of a single conifer is also very effective and particularly appealing in the autumn.

RIGHT *Berberis thunbergii atropurpurea:* height 20 cm (8 in); age 10 years. This bonsai was created from ordinary garden centre material.

SPECIES AND VARIETIES

Not all species are suitable for bonsai, as many tend to be very stiff growing and are thus difficult to shape. The best way to train such species is to start them from cuttings, when new growth can be melded into the desired positions. The evergreen species, such as the common *B. stenophyllas,* are very rarely used. Usually coloured species and varieties, and ones that make good autumn colour are chosen, such as Japanese barberry (*B. thunbergii*). Some of these can grow into very tall shrubs, and thus in the course of time have the potential to make good-quality bonsai with thick and solid trunks.

CARE

This is a species that is easy to care for. Until the roots are well established do not repot it. Some winter protection is needed, but other than that there are no special requirements. When pruned, both the stems and roots have an unusual, intense yellow inner colour.

LEFT Japanese barberry
(Berberis thunbergii): height
45 cm (18 in); age
approximately 35 years.
This bonsai was collected
from a garden hedge.

BETULA SPP. BIRCH

DESCRIPTION

The Silver birch is commonly planted in parks and gardens in preference to the Common birch, as it is a delicately foliaged small tree, with weeping branches and silvered bark that peels off in horizontal strips, displaying a rich undercolour. Old trees often have quite substantial trunks.

The leaves are small and delicate, making them an ideal subject for bonsai. They are alternate on the shoot, and deciduous, but rarely do they make very good autumn colours. Despite this fact, and the fact that they are common in Europe and Eastern Asia, they are seldom seen as a bonsai. They are hardly ever pictured in Japanese exhibition books, although they are listed in catalogues of species suitable for bonsai there. Perhaps it is because Birch grow quickly at first and in an erect manner, before exhibiting weeping branches, and when growing in an unwanted place are considered weeds. Their potential, however, is very good and in the course of time there should be some reasonable-quality specimens in the West.

BONSAI STYLES AND PRESENTATION

A good Birch bonsai should be light in appearance and informally styled. The bark should be of a silvery colour or show the typical shiny quality of a mature tree, depending on the species. Trees, whether single or in group plantings, should exhibit grace and elegance and not look stiff and stilted, but natural, with a soft appearance. Close inspection of quite young trees is likely to reveal catkins.

The pot will usually be of a light glazed colour. Single trees may well be planted in long, shallow pots, offset from the middle so that there is an empty expanse to one side of the tree. This helps to accentuate the grace

ABOVE European silver birch *(Betula verrucosa)* grown in the root-over-rock style; height 58 cm (23 in); age 10 years.

BELOW *Betulus*
verrucosa: height 51 cm
(20 in); age 12 years.

and delicacy of the specimen and give a feeling of spaciousness to the arrangement. Alternatively, Birch can be planted on a slab of rock.

SPECIES AND VARIETIES

There are two Birches that are likely to be used for bonsai in the West; the European silver birch or European white birch (*B. verrucosa*), with its graceful, weeping branches, and *B. pubescens*. For bonsai use there is not a lot to choose between them other than the colour of the bark, although there is a difference in leaf quality and shape when the two are compared; the former is hairless and

the shape is pointed rather than rounded. Grown under bonsai conditions it is not easy to reproduce the weeping effect or to get the bark to go white in the European silver birch.

CARE

Birch need to be grown in full sun and watered well. Other than that they have no special requirements; they are very sturdy subjects. Because their leaves are small the trees do not need to be defoliated, but if they are defoliated, their autumn leaf colour will be marginally improved and the time before leaf fall will be extended.

BUXUS SPP. BOX

DESCRIPTION

Box is a genus of usually small evergreen shrubs, although a few achieve treelike proportions. The leaves of box are small, which is an ideal attribute for a bonsai. They are shiny, but the flowers and fruit are not at all conspicuous. However, growth is stiff and angular so it is not easy to make acceptable-looking bonsai. Box should be more popular than it actually is, especially as it has been used for hedging for many years and consequently there must be many old hedges that would provide suitable bonsai material.

BONSAI STYLES AND PRESENTATIONS

When seen as a bonsai, a good specimen should not look as though it has just come out of a garden tub. It should show no hint of stiffness and angularity but be soft in form. A good specimen may well exhibit dead-wood effects that have been added deliberately so as to enhance the illusion of age. Trunks may even be split through to add to this effect. Such creations are likely to have been engineered by the more adventurous bonsai artists.

Box is an ideal subject to make into a twin-trunked tree, and it is happy to be grown with its roots over a rock or even clinging to a rock. Most specimens are likely to be very ordinary looking, lacking any great artistic appeal. The colour of the pot should be deep, and if glazed it should not appear too glossy.

SPECIES AND VARIETIES

There are only a small number of species in the *Buxus* genus. The Common box (*B. sempervirens*) is not too different from the Small-leaved or Japanese box (*B. microphylla*) in general habit and appearance. Both are available in a number of varieties, including ones with variegated leaves. One

ABOVE *Buxus sinica:* height 64 cm (25 in); age 180 years. A Chinese styled bonsai displays foliage arranged in cloud layers.

that is very frequently seen in American bonsai magazines and books is Kingsville dwarf box, which is a cultivar of *B. microphylla* 'Compacta'; this particular cultivar may not be available in Europe, at least at present. Those trees with a good glossy shine to the leaves are perhaps best, as they give the tree plenty of sparkle when it is in peak condition and on display.

CARE

Box needs to be protected from frosts in the winter, and for this reason some classify it as an indoor bonsai. Other than that it is an easy subject to grow. It needs regular thinning out of the foliage to get light into the inner branches to encourage back budding and to keep the shape compact. When the roots are confined, growth is slow and trunk thickening is almost nonexistent.

LEFT *Buxus sinica:* height 60cm (24 in); age 80 years. This delightful tree is titled 'A Frost in a Wealth of Green'.

CARPINUS SPP. HORNBEAM, IRONWOOD

DESCRIPTION

The Hornbeam is a very popular subject for bonsai, both in the West and in Japan. It is not one of the easiest subjects to create successfully because it is a quick grower and needs much attention in its early days to keep it under control. It is a tree that grows moderately tall and in an elegant manner. It is renowned for the silvery-purple coloured fluting of the bark on the trunk, which helps to distinguish it from the Beech (Fagus species – see pages 50 and 51 for comparison) with which it is often confused.

Hornbeam is a deciduous species. Its leaves are similar to the Beech, but are narrower and more distinctly veined. They grow alternately on the shoot, going in almost all directions. Its buds are also shorter than those of the Beech. Hornbeams on the whole do not make good autumn colour, although in a good year their leaves turn a good, rich yellow before falling early. The leaves burn easily when in full sun.

BONSAI STYLES AND PRESENTATION

Hornbeams are usually grown as formal or informal upright trees. They are also sometimes grown in small groves or groups. The foliage should be in perfect condition when on display, with no burned leaf margins; all damaged leaves should be removed beforehand. The tree should show structure rather than being just a dense head of foliage. The trunk should show the minimum of blemishes, but pruning cuts that seal over give the trunk the appearance of age and add to its character.

Containers will usually be glazed and shallow. Although deeper containers are sometimes seen, they are used specifically for horticultural reasons rather than purely for display purposes.

ABOVE Korean hornbeam *(Carpinus turczaninovii):* height 32 cm (13 in). This delightful group of saplings was originally imported from Japan and has been in training for five years.

BELOW Japanese hornbeam *(Carpinus japonica)*: height 30 cm (12 in) with a 90-cm (35-in) spread; age unknown. Grown in the horizontal or semi-cascade style, this bonsai is thought to be very old.

SPECIES AND VARIETIES

There are a number of Hornbeams spread across the Northern Hemisphere. In the West, the Common or European hornbeam (*C. betulus*) will usually be used. In Japan, the Loose-flowered hornbeam (*C. laxiflora*) is favoured. Korean hornbeam (*C. turczaninovii*) is a species that makes extremely good, rich and varied autumn colours; it makes a superior specimen when compared with the Common or European hornbeam but is not so easy to come by in the West.

CARE

Hornbeams need protection from the sun and the wind to ensure that the leaf margins do not get burned. They are sometimes defoliated to help keep the leaves small, but this inhibits the production of flowers, so should never be practised on a tree that has reached flowering and fruiting maturity. It is a species that does not like to be over-watered, but without sufficient water the possibility of leaf burn is increased. Constant grooming is needed to maintain the shape of the tree, as growth is long and vigorous and goes in every direction possible.

ABOVE Common
hornbeam *(Carpinus
betulus):* width 50 cm
(20 in); grown over a rock
in the semi-cascade style.
This tree was collected from
the wild as a young sapling
and has been in training for
seven years.

CEDRUS SPP. CEDAR

DESCRIPTION

This is a small genus of evergreen trees whose foliage is characterized by short spurs of growth, and at the tips the leaves are scattered around the shoot, with weeping ends. With age all Cedars growing in their native habitat make open structures with flat planes of foliage.

There are numerous other trees with the word cedar in their names that are not members of this genus, and this can add to confusion when identifying trees. Cedars are most likely to be confused with Larches, which are very similar in appearance (Larix species – see pages 60–62 for comparison), but the fact that Cedars are evergreen gives them away in the winter. On the whole, cedars are likely to be thinner stemmed when grown as bonsai than Larches, and the needle quality is different – those on Cedar look stiff rather than soft.

Cedars of any quality are not very often seen as bonsai, although as normal trees they are familiar to most people. When grown in open spaces they make impressive structures, often dominating the landscape.

BONSAI STYLES
AND PRESENTATION

Cedars are usually grown as formal upright bonsai to take advantage of their stately growing nature. They may also be seen in informal styles and are ideal for making into windswept trees. Sometimes they may be seen as twin trunks, split trunks, or with their roots over a rock, in clumps and group plantings. The commonly available Blue cedar is often seen growing in the free-form literati style, though usually not as a very good specimen.

Pots will usually be unglazed and in dull rather than bright colours, although the Blue cedar varieties will take a glazed pot.

SPECIES AND VARIETIES

There are only three species of Cedar commonly seen – Atlas cedar (*C. atlantica*). Cedar-of-Lebanon (*C. libani*) and Deodar (*C. deodara*) – but the Cyprus cedar (*C. brevifolia*) is sometimes used for bonsai. Frequently used for bonsai these days is the Blue atlas cedar (*C. atlantica glauca*), which is generally available in most garden centres. In Japan, Cedar-of-Lebanon is the most common.

CARE

Cedars are one of the more fussy subjects when grown as bonsai. They need to be kept on the dry side; overwatering results in the needles turning yellow. They do not like being root-pruned too often; this should only be done when absolutely necessary. Sometimes repotting can cause all of the needles to drop. Fortunately if this happens a new flush quickly follows. As a species they tend not to thicken very much when in a bonsai pot, and for this reason really impressive specimens will have been grown in the open ground for some time before being converted into a bonsai.

Heavy pruning scars seal over very slowly, if at all, and if major branches are removed, dead stubs are usually left. These are called *jin* (pronounced gin), and they help to add to the illusion of age. Sometimes they are deliberately created.

OPPOSITE Cyprus
cedar *(Cedrus brevifolia):*
height 33 cm (13 in); age
approximately 12 years.
This young grafted tree was
obtained as nursery stock
and is displayed with a
Cotoneaster accent
planting.

ABOVE Atlas cedar
(Cedrus atlantica): height
37 cm (15 in); age
approximately 20 years.

CHAENOMELES SPP. FLOWERING QUINCE

DESCRIPTION

Flowering quince makes a delightful show of colour during the early part of the year, and this can be any time from January onwards, depending where the specimen is located. The flowers, usually reds and pinks with yellow centres, form before leaf break and continue for a long time thereafter, even when leaves have fully formed. In some species flowering is sporadic, giving a poor show of colour at any one time over an extended flowering period. Fruit, when it is allowed to form, is yellow and large.

Flowering quince are shrubs that come from China and Japan. They are commonly referred to as Japonica and are extensively used as a garden plant, trained up the sides of the house by the front door. They are similar to, but distinct from, the true Quince (the genus *Pseudocydonia*), which if seen as a bonsai is usually in a more conventional tree shape.

BONSAI STYLES AND PRESENTATION

Quality bonsai Flowering quince, of which there are many in Japan, have usually been dug up from gardens and potted up to make into a bonsai. Almost invariably they are not tree-shaped, but look like a massive and extensive stump from which short shoots arise to carry the showy flowers.

Sometimes flowers of different colours will be found on the same tree. This is achieved by grafting on another variety at various places. A *few* different coloured flowers do not look very out of place if the colour distinctions are not too jarring. Whites may work well with pale pinks, but the result looks artificial if white is mixed with an intense red.

When grown in pots, flowering quince thicken their trunks very slowly, if at all; thus many Flowering quince bonsai likely to be seen will be thin trunked and carrying just a few flowers dotted here and there. Where trunks are thin they may be presented as cascades or made into small clumps and groupings. The literati style is also used extensively. Very small *mame* specimens make enjoyable novelties when just carrying one flower, and they can be used for display with a larger bonsai such as a Pine or Juniper. Flowering quince, if displayed in the winter, may well have one or two fruits deliberately and judiciously hung on the tree.

Pots are usually glazed and in subdued colours so as not to clash with the colour of the flowers. Sometimes they may be highly decorated, especially when used for the larger-sized trees.

SPECIES AND VARIETIES

Only a few of the Flowering quince species are used for bonsai, but among these there are many cultivars from which to choose, including *C. speciosa* 'Nivalis' and *C. speciosa* 'Rosea Plena'. Care should be taken to differentiate this species from the true Quince, *Pseudocydonia,* which is also used as bonsai and commonly called Chinese quince in bonsai books.

CARE

Flowering quince should be fed to encourage flowering. After flowering is over the tree should be deadheaded, and periodic checks should be made to ensure that no fruit has formed to sap the tree of vital energy.

OPPOSITE Flowering quince (Chaenomeles variety): height 24 cm (9 in). This young bonsai was created from a garden-centre stock plant.

CHAMAECYPARIS SPP. FALSE CYPRESS

DESCRIPTION

False cypresses are evergreen conifers. They are often confused with true Cypress, Junipers, and a few other species of tree with similar compact, scalelike foliage. There are a number of other species that have the word cypress in their names that are neither true nor False cypress, such as the Swamp cypress (*Taxodium distichum*).

Because False cypress is a species readily and cheaply available from nurseries and garden centres, it is often used for bonsai, although it is only the Hinoki cypress (*C. obtusa*) that really measures up to the standards required to make a quality bonsai. Many of the species do not make compact foliage pads, and branches and twigs grow faster with an open rather than compact structure. Others make dense domes of foliage which give them an artificial appearance if used for bonsai.

BONSAI STYLES AND PRESENTATION

Many False cypress tend not to make good bonsai when grown singly, and for this reason they are often grouped together, making impressive groves and forests of upright trees. In any such arrangement the silhouette of the grouping should exhibit triangularity. Small groves may have the same trunk caliper for all of the trees, but larger plantings will need trees that give the appearance of old age and youth through a variation in height and trunk thickness.

A good single specimen should show the basic branch structure, and it should look like a tree whose foliage birds and butterflies can flit through. There should be no sign of any dead foliage on the tree, although close inspection may reveal inner pockets of old foliage overlooked when the tree was groomed for display.

SPECIES AND VARIETIES

Hinoki cypress (*C. obtusa*) is used to make a classical Cypress bonsai. It is available in a number of varieties and cultivars, many of which have better-quality foliage than the parent, such as *C. obtusa* 'Nana Gracilis'. Unfortunately this particular one tends to grow slowly, loosing inner foliage which it does not replace. It then becomes straggly and has to be redesigned into a literati style tree. Others used are Sawara cypress (*C. pisifera*), and the cultivar *C. lawsoniana* 'Ellwoodii'; both have compact foliage and branches packed close together.

CARE

False cypresses demand a lot of attention. They need to be given some wind protection, particularly in the winter if they become frozen up for any length of time. In the summer they need some shade, especially group plantings in shallow trays. New growth should be pinched out and foliage periodically thinned. If this is not done, a dense head of foliage will develop and the bonsai will soon start to look like any container-grown tree.

BELOW Hinoki cypress (*Chamaecyparis obtusa*): height 55 cm (22 in) with a spread of 90 cm (35 in); age unknown. This group, growing in a piece of sandstone, was imported from Japan 30 years ago.

LEFT Sawara cypress (*Chamaecyparis pisifera* 'Boulevard'): height 90 cm (35 in). This small group was created with young trees obtained as ordinary garden centre stock.

OPPOSITE Sawara cypress variety: height 120 cm (47 in); age probably less than ten years. This bonsai was created only six months before this photograph was taken and is as yet an unrefined specimen.

CORNUS SPP. DOGWOOD

DESCRIPTION

Most people know Dogwoods by their bright-coloured young stems that provide some winter colour. Not all Dogwoods have such stems, however; it is mainly the shrubby ones originating in North America that are so colourful. Those of European and Asian origin tend to grow into small trees, often with multi-stems, and it is these that make good bonsai specimens. Dogwoods are deciduous, with leaves which are distinctively veined, in pairs. The leaves and new shoots tend to be parallel with the stem on which they grow.

Flowers form on the bare wood before leaf break in some species, while in others they come out in midyear. They are not very showy and tend to be few, but in the case of *C. kousa* there are white bracts that surround the flower, giving a very distinctive appearance. The bright-coloured fruit varies from small cherrylike berries to those resembling small strawberries.

BONSAI STYLES AND PRESENTATION

Dogwood is not a species to make into formal trees, but it is ideal for informal styles, particularly those with two or more stems, and is sometimes grown in the cascading style. When multistemmed it should not look stiff but be soft and feminine in appearance.

The best time of year for display depends on the species. Some are best when they are in flower. Others are most striking in their autumn clothes, when the bright fruit glistens with the sometimes quite fiery autumnal tints. Pots will usually be glazed, and quite often a round or square pot will be used when the tree is grown in the multitrunk style.

Sometimes the coloured stem species are seen in bonsai pots. But even in winter they do not look very appealing, and a massive and densely crowded group is needed to make an interesting display worthy of being called a bonsai. Even then the shoots need to have been precisely trained to get an acceptable arrangement, and such training needs to be repeated every other year to regenerate the fresh, coloured growth.

SPECIES AND VARIETIES

In Japan, *C. kousa* is the main species of Dogwood used for bonsai. It is also used as a street tree there and is renowned for the rich range of autumn colours that it makes. The Cornelian cherry (*C. mas*) of European origin makes poor autumn colour in comparison, but even so it can be an intense reddish purple if the right combination of environmental factors induce early leaf drop.

CARE

Dogwoods need to have some wind and sun protection, otherwise their leaf margins will become burned, and this is then likely to impair their autumn colours. Bright sun and frosty nights are, however, required for good autumn colour, otherwise growth continues, and when the leaves drop they may still be green.

Feeding has to be done with care, to control new growth. New wood takes a long time to ripen, and growth made after midsummer will mean that winter protection is essential. Late new growth may also inhibit the onset of colouration in the autumn, which is not good for the health of the tree.

OPPOSITE Cornelian cherry *(Cornus mas)* grown in the twin-trunk style; height 48 cm (19 in); age approximately 8 years.

COTONEASTER SPP.

DESCRIPTION

The small-leaved Cotoneasters are not only delightful deciduous shrubs when growing over a garden wall, they are equally attractive when grown as bonsai. They are usually angular in growing habit, and creep slowly but surely where they want to.

Cotoneasters are far from being a classical bonsai subject, despite being used extensively for bonsai in the West and Japan. The small leaves of *C. horizontalis* turn beautiful shades of red and orange in the autumn before they fall. Sometimes the leaves do not fall together but gradually so that there is a constant change of colour over the growing season as the old leaves are slowly replaced. Small flowers come in the spring and these lead on to red berries in the autumn. Cotoneasters are native to mountainous areas in Europe, Asia and Africa.

C. horizontalis, with its herringbone growth, is familiar in the West and is the species that is commercially produced in Japan as bonsai. Strangely, this species is not typical of cotoneasters, which as a whole have much longer and narrow leaves. It is imported in a range of sizes and qualities and is often shaped with a series of S bends in the trunk. They are usually under heavy wiring that will need instant removal.

BONSAI STYLES
AND PRESENTATION

There is hardly a time when Cotoneasters cannot be shown: when in flower, leaf, in berry, or when the leaves are turning colour. *C. horizontalis* is ideal for making into small-scale bonsai, called *mame,* and some that are just a few inches high may well be only a few years old. A really old *mame* Cotoneaster will be well buttressed at the base.

They can be made into almost any informal style, including horizontals and cascades.

ABOVE *Cotoneaster horizontalis:* height 33 cm (13 in); age approximately 20 years. This bonsai, in the informal upright style, was imported from Japan.

LEFT *Cotoneaster
horizontalis:* height 25 cm
(10 in); age over 25 years.
This tree, planted against a
rock, was collected from the
owner's front garden five
years earlier.

BELOW *Cotoneaster horizontalis:* height 25 cm (10 in). The arrangement is made up of young seedlings.

They can be arranged in groups. They go well on or with rocks, and sometimes they are used as ground cover plants for large-scale rock or slab plants or other bonsai.

Pots are usually glazed, and deep greens and blues are sympathetic with the colour of the leaves and the fruit in autumn.

SPECIES AND VARIETIES

Although it is not typical, *C. horizontalis,* (Rock cotoneaster or Rockspray as it is generally known in North America) is most widely used for bonsai. A typical Cotoneaster makes a spreading upright bush, with open branches and glossy, elliptical leaves, which is far removed from *C. horizontalis,* with its small leaves and herringbone pattern of branches. Some of these make ideal bonsai

but need to be styled with height in mind, rather than trying to make a small compact and squat specimen which is ideal for *C. horizontalis. C. microphyllus* is similar to *C. horizontalis* but has smaller leaves that are not as colourful in the autumn. It is also far less hardy.

CARE

Cotoneasters are easy to grow. They need no special care, except to watch for various moths that like to get in their foliage and lay their eggs there. To maintain flowering and fruiting, Cotoneasters need to be fed well. Most do not need winter protection, and new growth starts very early in the year, before midwinter in warmer regions.

CRATAEGUS SPP. HAWTHORN

DESCRIPTION

Hawthorn is a widespread species of small tree, and as the name implies it is armed with thorns. It is renowned for the quality and amount of its flowers, which may be single or double, and range from pure white to intense red. It does not flower until it is about 20 years old, so if grown from seed patience is required. The bark of old trees is deeply furrowed, and when grown in parks and open spaces, the trees quite naturally take on interesting shapes without the intervention of man.

The leaves are distinctive – alternate on the shoot and usually deeply incised. The trees are comparatively small and thus ideal as bonsai subjects. The fruit, known as haws, is in the form of berries and is usually red or orange, although some species produce yellow fruit.

BONSAI STYLES AND PRESENTATION

As growth is very angular, many stilted and rigid-looking bonsai Hawthorns may be seen, but a good bonsai must look quite natural. It should look like a miniature tree, even though designed to show off its flowers. It is more likely to be exhibited when in flower or in the autumn when the haws have ripened, either before or after the leaves have fallen, but before the fruit has fallen. A good-quality specimen could well be a delight when out of leaf because it is a species that quickly makes very good branch ramification.

The style in which it is grown can vary enormously, from very formal upright trees right through to full cascades. Often specimens will be grown in the literati style, one that does not conform to any set of preconceived rules other than having a thin, long trunk, be spartan of foliage, and usually be housed in a small, round pot. Hawthorn is an

ABOVE A species of Crataegus (Hawthorn) grown as a small group of three trees and showing good autumn colouration; height 48 cm (19 in); age 18 years.

ideal subject to make into semi- and flowing cascades. Pots will be glazed more often than not, whatever the style.

SPECIES AND VARIETIES

There are very many species of Hawthorn, but only a few are commonly available. Those likely to be encountered are Cockspur thorn (*C. crus-galli*), *C. monogyna* and *C. oxyacantha*. For bonsai, those species and varieties renowned for their flowering qualities are used; Paul's Scarlet (*C. monogyna*) is of particular note. In Japan Japanese hawthorn (*C. cuneata*) is commonly used.

CARE

Hawthorn needs considerable attention to keep its growth under control; shoots grow in all directions and tangled masses can quickly form. Sucker growth needs to be removed as it forms. A feeding schedule that encourages flower and fruit production should be maintained. Precaution needs to be taken against insect and fungal attack.

OPPOSITE Common hawthorn *(Crataegus mongyna)*: span 42 cm (17 in); age over 50 years. In the literati style, this specimen was grown from collected material and has been in training for 6 years.

ABOVE RIGHT Common hawthorn *(Crataegus monogyna)*: height 20 cm (8 in); age 16 years. Grown in the informal upright style, this bonsai was started from seed.

RIGHT Common hawthorn *(Crataegus monogyna)*.

CRYPTOMERIA SPP.

DESCRIPTION

Cryptomeria is often referred to as Japanese cedar, but it is not a true cedar because it is not a member of the *Cedrus* genus of trees. It is a native of both Japan and China where it is regularly used for bonsai. Cryptomerias make tall, narrow trees with a solid buttress at the base, and they have reddish-brown bark that peels off in long strips down the length of the trunk. In Japan it is an important ornamental tree, and it is often found growing by the sides of temples, where specimens up to 60 m (200 ft) in height may sometimes be seen.

Its foliage is a light but bright green-blue colour in the growing season, but it turns reddish-brown for the winter, making it look as though the tree is dead. It is also slightly prickly to the touch. The broad, needlelike evergreen leaves are densely packed around the shoot, which is not really visible. The branches form in whorls, spread, and eventually droop, giving a particularly aged look to the tree.

BONSAI STYLES AND PRESENTATION

Cryptomeria is usually grown as an upright tree with the branches either horizontal or drooping. The foliage is often trained up and elevated above the branch, giving it something of an artificial appearance and making it look somewhat like the underside of a mushroom that has been turned inside out. However designed, the foliage should be meticulously groomed before being displayed, otherwise it will look very unkempt. The spread of foliage is usually narrow, and when it is, the container used is often quite squat. Sometimes Cryptomeria are grown in small groups and forest arrangements, but the trees will always have an upright, stately stance.

To make a good specimen the trunk must have the peeling bark, and the branches must be reasonably spaced to show a definite structure rather than a densely clothed tree. Unwanted branches are likely to be left as short stubs of dead wood – *jins* – and sometimes they may appear where a branch might have been expected to be.

SPECIES AND VARIETIES

Cryptomeria only comes as the species *C. japonica,* but there are a host of cultivars, a few of which are better suited to bonsai than others, such as *C. japonica* 'Viminalis', or one of the dwarf cultivars, *C. japonica* 'Zuisho' and *C. japonica* 'Tokyo'.

CARE

To keep this species in good condition much attention has to be given to pinching out new growth with the fingers; it is a time-consuming task. Pruning the foliage with scissors should be avoided since this causes the foliage to turn brown at the tips. Some shade is needed in the summer, and plenty of water should be given. Mist with water to discourage red spider mite, which likes to nest on the tree and damage the foliage. Winter protection against late frosts is advisable.

ABOVE A dwarf species
of Japanese cedar
*(Cryptomeria japonica
yatsubusa)* in a group
planting and under training
for six months; height 70 cm
(28 in); ages 4 to 8 years.

EHRETIA SPP.

DESCRIPTION

This is a very small genus of tropical tree that will also be referred to in books under the name *Carmona;* it should now be correctly described as *Ehretia.* Ehretias make small trees, usually with a light grey bark which forms an interesting crackled surface with age. They are either evergreen or deciduous, depending on the species, with shiny dark green leaves, and they form panicles of small white flowers in early summer.

In the West they are not usually hardy in the evergreen forms and when used for bonsai are considered an indoor subject. The species Fukien Tea (*E. buxifolia*) is extensively used for making into bonsai in China and Southeast Asia. Although also native to Japan, this species is surprisingly rarely used for bonsai there.

BONSAI STYLES AND PRESENTATION

Fukien Tea can be made into almost any style of bonsai. Many magnificent bonsai specimens abound in Southeast Asia; it is admirably suited to the Chinese approach to bonsai, and is sometimes also seen in the literati style as well as planted as groups. Fukien Tea is also a favoured subject for bonsai in Hong Kong and China, where it is not unusual to see it displayed with all of the leaves removed, revealing the underlying form of the tree.

SPECIES AND VARIETIES

E. buxifolia (formerly *Carmona microphylla*), commonly called Fukien Tea, is evergreen with small box-like leaves, and is the only species likely to be encountered for bonsai

use. The deciduous species of *E. dicksonii* and *E. thrysiflora* survive without any special sheltering or frost protection and could be used for bonsai.

CARE

As the leaves turn yellow they should be removed to neaten the appearance of the tree. If the foliage takes on a general yellowish sickly look, this will be due to overwatering. Repot using a freer-draining compost.

Ehretia are quick growing so new shoots should be constantly pinched back. Daily mist spraying will be appreciated, but use only distilled water as tap water encourages a build-up of lime on the leaves, making the plant look anaemic and unsightly. Frequent misting will also help deter pests such as red spider mites.

In the summer trees should be placed out of doors in a fairly bright spot that catches either the morning or evening sun. This will encourage the trees to build up strength for the winter. Indoors they should be located in a bright and draught-free spot where they only get sun for an hour or so each day.

LEFT *Ehretia buxifolia:* height 115 cm (45 in); age approximately 50 years. This species is an indoor bonsai subject in the West.

OPPOSITE Fukien Tea *(Ehretia buxifolia):* spread 135 cm (53 in); age 50 years.

FAGUS SPP. BEECH

DESCRIPTION

Beech are classical bonsai subjects. Their leaves are a little on the large size, although they do reduce in size naturally so long as the tree is only repotted infrequently. As a genus of trees they are found in both hemispheres. In the Southern Hemisphere they should not be confused with the so-called Southern beeches; they are a different genus of tree entirely.

Under ideal growing conditions Beech make massive trees with erect growing branches. Sometimes they are densely clothed with foliage; other times they have open, spreading branches, depending whether they are grown in isolation of other trees or in a forest setting. Beech tend to make a very heavy shade where little can grow underneath them. They are deciduous and are easily recognized by their long, brown cigar-shaped buds. Their leaves, however, can be confused with those of Hornbeams (Carpinus species – see pages 29–31), but the simplest way to differentiate them is by inspection of the buds or through the conspicuously silvery veining on the trunks of Hornbeams. The bark of the Common or European beech (*F. sylvatica*) is smooth and grey.

BONSAI STYLES AND PRESENTATION

Beech are well suited for training into either formal, upright-style bonsai or ones that are a little less formal, with an asymmetric or nearly asymmetric outline. Young trees may sometimes be formed into groups. The trunk should be unblemished, showing no pruning scars. It should be bright and uniform in colour, sometimes even brilliant white. Closer inspection may even reveal that the trunk and branches have been whitewashed, but there will always be tell-tale signs to give this away.

Pots will usually be glazed and shallow. Trees that do not have a very substantial trunk may be planted in long containers, considerably off to one side of the pot. They may be displayed in winter to show off the fine ramification of their branches and buds. Sometimes they may even be holding dead leaves. When in the growing season all leaf margins should be in perfect condition.

SPECIES AND VARIETIES

There are only a few species of Beech used for bonsai. The Common or European beech (*F. sylvatica*) is used in the West; its equivalent in Japan is the White or Japanese beech (*F. crenata*), which is named for the colour of its trunk, and hence the reason why it is sometimes whitewashed to enhance its appearance. It is better than the Common or European beech for bonsai because it has slightly smaller leaves. The cut-leaved species are only infrequently used, but both the green-leaved and purple beeches will frequently be encountered in *F. sylvatica* and in *F. sylvatica atropurpurea*.

CARE

Beeches are easy to grow as bonsai. They are not fussy about their conditions, but when grown in shallow pots need to be watered well, especially under hot and windy conditions when leaf margins can become burned. Defoliation has to be undertaken almost immediately after the new leaves for the year have hardened. Beeches attract aphids on the underside of their leaves, so a constant lookout is needed for them.

BELOW *Fagus sylvatica:*
height 92 cm (36 in); age 10
years. At the time this
photograph was taken the
tree had been under
training as a bonsai for
two years.

ABOVE Common or
European beech *(Fagus
sylvatica):* height 65 cm
(26 in); age approximately
50 years. This bonsai was
created from material
collected from a forest
plantation.

FICUS SPP. FIG

DESCRIPTION

Figs used for bonsai come mainly from tropical and subtropical climes, so they have to be treated as indoor bonsai. Some Figs are deciduous; others have bright shiny, leathery evergreen leaves. There are several hundred species, few of which are ever seen outside of the tropics. The fruit is not always edible, and many of the species make aerial roots which are sometimes featured in a bonsai. Some Figs are sometimes referred to as Banyan trees.

BONSAI STYLES AND PRESENTATION

Figs can be made into almost any conceivable style because they shape easily. They are ideal for growing over a piece of rock or for growing in dense clumps with the stems close together. The roots can be exposed, and in the case of the Weeping fig will produce aerial roots that add to the effect. It is best to train the roots rather than leave them to grow as they please. Aged specimens can be made into very impressive trees and are expensive to acquire.

Sometimes different varieties of Weeping figs may be grouped together so that both unvariegated and variegated leaves are displayed together.

SPECIES AND VARIETIES

The Weeping fig, or Benjamin tree, (F. benjamina) is commonly available and is likely to be widely seen as a bonsai. It is evergreen and the stem is very supple, allowing it to be trained easily into interesting shapes. The Common fig, or Edible fig tree, is F. carica, but its leaves are far too large for bonsai. The Banyan tree (F. microcarpa) is sometimes seen as quite an old bonsai specimen. Other species encountered as bonsai include F. salicifolia and F. retusa.

CARE

Figs need to be kept out of draughts when indoors, and for the most part like to be in a place where there is a constant warm temperature with plenty of humidity and light. Spray plants daily with water or keep them on a tray of gravel filled with water to provide a humid microclimate. The Edible fig is of Mediterranean origin and can be overwintered in a cool greenhouse, but all other varieties need to be indoors.

Growth is quite vigorous, and over-large leaves should be removed regularly. Sometimes they are stripped of all their leaves, so long as the tree has been well fed beforehand and is in a healthy condition. The fast growth quickly produces an aged appearance. Examine routinely for scale insects and treat them as soon as they are spotted.

ABOVE Willow-leaved fig (Ficus salicifolia), grown as a forest planting. A native of Florida, this species is a very popular bonsai subject there, as the climate – high temperatures and humidity – encourages the species to develop very rapidly, producing a sizeable trunk girth in a relatively short time.

OPPOSITE Ficus retusa: height 85 cm (33 in); age 174 years. This is a Chinese bonsai of considerable note named 'The Coiling Dragon'.

GINKGO SPP.

DESCRIPTION

Ginkgo is a deciduous species of tree in a group all of its own. It is sometimes described as a conifer, and although it is closely related to conifers, it is not a conifer as such. It is a tree that in the past populated much of the world, as evidenced by its fossil remains, but it is now mainly cultivated for garden use and is grown as a street tree in Japan. It makes a narrow, upright tree that only in old age starts to spread and look old.

Its leaves are quite distinctive and will never be confused with those of any other species. The leaves are of two types: fan shaped, with veins running through them like the spokes of a fan; and deeply incised at the centre. In the autumn they change to a beautiful butter yellow colour but quickly fall, thus only having a short period of glory.

BONSAI STYLES
AND PRESENTATION

Ginkgos do not lend themselves readily to being made into a great range of bonsai styles, due to their erect growing habit. They tend to be seen as dense heads of foliage on upright stems with little other form. Good specimens should have foliage of a fine and not coarse quality. If seen in the autumn they may well be displayed for a brief period with their butter-yellow leaves, or alternatively they may be seen displaying fruit.

Ginkgos are traditionally displayed in deep blue glazed pots, sometimed called export blue. The trunks may look gnarled and blemished, but this is quite natural unless clearly caused by pruning and is a sign of maturity. The trunk should be powerful and squat in relation to the height; it should not appear to be tall and slim. Neither should it look like a truncheon, top heavy with foliage.

When on display the leaves should be a clear green and not appear leathery nor

BELOW *Ginkgo biloba:* height 80 cm (32 in); age approximately 90 years. This ancient subject has been grown as a clump.

show any signs of lime marks, which will usually be left after having been sprayed with tap water.

SPECIES AND VARIETIES

There is only one species in this genus, and it has just a few varieties, most of which are rarely seen. The Ginkgo commonly encountered in the West is not suitable for making into good bonsai; the leaf is of poor quality, being dull green and of leathery appearance. Traditionally the cultivar *G. biloba* 'Chichi Icho' is used in Japan, or one of the other varieties renowned for their fruit-bearing qualities. (Fruit is in the form of nuts.)

Sometimes natural variegation takes place in the leaf, and if it does, that portion of the tree can be layered off, so long as the overall design of the tree is not spoiled by doing so.

CARE

Ginkgo does not need a lot of looking after other than regular pruning to keep the shape compact. Trees should be fed either to encourage fruiting, or to encourage the production of stalactitic-type aerial roots that only form on old and large trees which are rarely seen in the West.

RIGHT *Ginkgo biloba:*
height 80 cm (32 in); age
150 years — a prize winning
Chinese bonsai of
impressive stature.

JUNIPERUS SPP. JUNIPER

DESCRIPTION

Along with Pines and Maples this is one of the top three species of tree used for bonsai. Junipers are widely distributed throughout the world, naturally lending themselves to bonsai. No bonsai collection is complete without a number of them and in a variety of styles. Some of the Junipers make very large trees – often over 30 m (100 ft) – but it is usually the dwarf varieties and cultivars that are used for bonsai. These can make very impressive shrubs, with bark that looks aged from an early stage.

Junipers are unusual in that they have foliage of two types. Some only have what is called juvenile foliage, which is awl shaped (needlelike), while others have a mixture of types with one form predominating, depending on the species. The adult foliage is fine and scalelike and more desirable. The colour of the foliage ranges over the greens, from steely blue-green to light green, sometimes with gold or silvery hues. Berries come in a variety of colours.

All of the older Juniper bonsai in Japan have been collected from the wild and is at least 50, if not 100, years or more old before it is transferred to a bonsai pot. Only those exhibiting character and much dead wood for featuring are selected and developed into bonsai. Needle juniper (*J. rigida*), which only has juvenile-type foliage, is extensively grown commercially.

BONSAI STYLES AND PRESENTATION

Junipers can be made into all of the known bonsai styles, and may well feature much dead wood. Some of the dead-wood effects will have been created naturally but are enhanced artificially, or even completely man-made. Dead wood that is brilliant white has been bleached, perhaps with some

ABOVE *Juniperus chinensis* 'San Jose' is a dwarf form of Chinese juniper. This example is growing on a rock; height 51 cm (20 in); age 15 years.

ABOVE Common
juniper *(Juniperus
communis)* grown in the
cascade style and exhibiting
dead-wood effects formed
naturally while growing
in the wild.

LEFT California juniper
(Juniperus californica) with
an impressive driftwood
effect.

acrylic white paint added to the bleach mix. In Japan there are bonsai artists who carve and hollow out the trunks of old specimens into real works of art, spending many days doing so with the aid of several assistants.

Foliage should all appear to be of the same type; it should not be mixed. Needle juniper (*J. rigida*) is best displayed when new growth has started, to bring the otherwise dull, old foliage to life. Pots will usually be in subdued coloured pots of browns and beiges, but not green, unless of a distinctively different shade from that of the foliage.

SPECIES AND VARIETIES

Junipers come in many species, and it is usually the varieties of *J. chinensis*, *J. recurva*, *J. sabina* and *J. virginiana* that are made into bonsai, as well as some of the media hybrids. Not all varieties are suitable, but with so many to choose from, the compact-growing and fine-foliaged forms are best. The classic Juniper subjects in Japan and the West are *J. chinensis sargentii* (known as Shimpaku juniper in the United States), and Needle juniper (*J. rigida*). In the United States the native California juniper (*J. californica*) is collected extensively, and there are now many impressive bonsai specimens of it.

CARE

The maintenance of a Juniper is quite easy, so long as the required pinching is done during the growing season and the foliage is thinned in the early part of the autumn to let in light. With those trees that make both juvenile and adult foliage it is essential to pluck out the growing ends of the juvenile to encourage it to form adult growth.

ABOVE *Juniperus sabina:* height 100 cm (39 in); age 150 years. This bonsai was created from material collected from the wild in the triple-trunk style.

LEFT Chinese juniper *(Juniperus chinensis):* height 75 cm (30 in); age probably in excess of 70 years. This is a Japanese import in the informal upright style.

RIGHT *Juniperus
chinensis* 'Blaauw': height
23 cm (9 in); age 10 years.
This is an impressive small-
scale bonsai created by
wrapping a young tree
around an old piece of
dead wood.

LARIX SPP. LARCH

DESCRIPTION

Larch is a deciduous conifer and a very popular subject for bonsai. This is not just because starter material is easy to obtain and trunks thicken quickly, but also because of how interesting it is both in the spring and autumn. There is nothing more appealing than to see the new growth burst forward in a delightful fresh green while the needles are still small. In the autumn the foliage turns either a golden or a pinkish yellow colour before dropping. Throughout the winter the tree can be enjoyed just for its sheer form, especially when it has a few small cones dotted here and there.

Cones are small and egg-shaped and are thus well in proportion to the tree. They also remain for several years before falling. Coning normally commences when trees are just a few years old, but some trees are more reluctant than others to start flowering. Growth is in the form of a rosette raised on a small spur, with terminal buds making extension growth. The flowers are interesting and come before new growth starts; in some species they are quite significant.

BONSAI STYLES AND PRESENTATION

Larch lend themselves to being created in many styles but are best when grown informally. Sometimes they are grown on slabs of rock, and when they are, the ground cover used must be good and interesting. If styled as a small group, the group will need to be broken up after a time because Larch thickens relatively quickly even when grown under bonsai conditions. Foliage must show no signs of browning, and should not hang down either from the tips or the undersides of the branches. Branch planes should be clearly defined with uncluttered space between them.

OPPOSITE TOP
Japanese larch *(Larix leptolepis);* height 65 cm (26 in); age approximately 40 years.

LEFT European larch *(Larix decidua):* height 80cm (32 in); age 30 years. This group planting is displayed in an autumn setting showing interesting ground cover.

OPPOSITE BOTTOM
European larch *(Larix decidua):* height 122 cm (48 in); age 25 years. The bonsai is displaying flowers and cones from the previous year.

Glazed pots are sometimes used, as Larch is a more flamboyant species than most of the other conifers.

SPECIES AND VARIETIES

There are only a few species of Larch. Those usually used for bonsai are either the Japanese larch (*L. leptolepis*) or European larch (*L. decidua*). In winter the Japanese Larch is reddish in appearance, and the European is yellow.

CARE

Larch needs some shade in the summer to prevent the leaves from burning, particularly if it is to be shown before the autumn. Feeding should be done to encourage fruiting and the formation of the cones, which can give even very young and insubstantial trees an aged appearance. Larch is particularly hardy and very resilient as a bonsai; it needs no winter protection.

ABOVE Larix species: height 65 cm (26 in); age approximately 50 years. When this specimen was collected from the wild the top was already dead.

LEFT Japanese larch (*Larix leptolepis*): height 52 cm (20 in); age 25 years. This tree was grown from seed in an extreme sloping style.

LONICERA SPP. HEDGE HONEYSUCKLE

DESCRIPTION

Honeysuckles are best known for their climbing habit and delightfully perfumed flowers. Not all are climbers, though; there are also shrubby species that are used for making dense hedges. All have small, neat, shiny green leaves with dense foliage. Flowers come very early in the year and are usually yellow but insignificant, and go on to make small and dark-coloured berries that often go unnoticed.

Hedge honeysuckles are evergreen or nearly so, and only achieve heights of a few feet. They make thick trunks and have a light, fawn-coloured bark that peels off in strips, revealing a smooth, light-coloured underbark. Because of this peeling habit they look quite old when only a few years of age. The growth is erect and stiff, and some expertise is needed to design a good bonsai and then maintain it.

BONSAI STYLES AND PRESENTATION

Due to their growing habit, Hedge honeysuckles have to be designed in informal styles, from uprights through to spreading cascades. To make a good bonsai the stiff aspect can either be softened by building curves into both the trunk and branches, or alternatively the male stature can be exploited. In the latter case there may be much dead wood included as part of the design, especially if an old specimen has been dug up out of a hedge to make into a bonsai. When dead-wood effects are included the natural colour of the wood is best featured, rather than making it brilliant white through the application of lime-sulphur bleach. Foliage pads should be kept compact. Substantial-trunked specimens will invariably be from collected material. It is a subject that can be designed to have an oriental look about it, and often many Hedge

ABOVE A species of Hedge honeysuckle, *Lonicera nitida:* girth 25 cm (10 in) at the base; age approximately 65 years. This tree was collected from the owner's hedge two years earlier.

honeysuckle bonsai will be of Chinese appearance. Sometimes they will be seen in the free-form literati style.

They look good in highly glazed pots. Deep blues in particular are very effective, especially for the golden variegated varieties, so long as the glaze is not absolutely uniform.

SPECIES AND VARIETIES

One of the main species used in bonsai is *L. nitida,* which has plain, deep green, shiny leaves, and often in the commonly available cultivar, *L. nitida* 'Baggesens's Gold', which has gold and orange-yellow hues in its deep green leaves. Another species is *L. pileata,* which has insignificant berries of a translucent violet and comes into growth very early in the year.

CARE

They are quite hardy, but in times of heavy frosts can lose most of their foliage unless winter protection is given. Any lost foliage soon regenerates in the spring. Considerable thinning out is needed each year, particularly of fine dead twigs. The long, quick-growing shoots also need to be pinched back regularly to keep the shape compact.

LEFT *Lonicera nitida:*
height 70 cm (28 in); age
indeterminate; showing
dead-wood effects — *jins.*

MALUS SPP. CRAB APPLE

DESCRIPTION

Crab apples, like azaleas, are one of the premier flowering species used for bonsai. Most Crab apples are fairly floriferous and highly scented. There is quite a variation in their flowering capacities and the quality of the fruit produced. The leaves of this decidu-ous species are comparatively small and are just opening when the flowers come in the spring.

In Japan there are many excellent-quality bonsai. Many that are created for export are propagated by air-layering 5-cm (2-in) diameter pieces of material from a stock tree that has reached flowering maturity.

BONSAI STYLES AND PRESENTATION

Crab apples are usually designed to show off their flowers and fruit. When displayed for their flowers, these should be in perfect con-dition; as they start to go over, they should be removed, or the tree taken out of display altogether. When in fruit the tree should not be too densely packed, and all fruit should be in perfect condition, whether there is still some leaf on the tree or not. Fruit that has dropped should not be left on the surface.

It is normal to design flowering bonsai with a view to showing off the flowers rather than to creating an interesting tree shape. But all too frequently this is used as an excuse for an ill-designed arrangement. The best of both worlds can be had with some of the smaller-leaved Crab apples, for they make ideal foliage and flowering bonsai.

Crab apples will usually be planted in a glazed pot of a colour that shows off the flowers or fruit. Pots need to be on the deep side, as Crab apples must have plenty of space for their roots. Ideally a different pot is needed for each of the two display periods: flowering and fruiting.

ABOVE A species of Malus (Crab apple): height 51 cm (20 in); age 30 years.

SPECIES AND VARIETIES

There are not many species of Crab apple but plenty of varieties, many of which are used for bonsai. One of particular note because of its very small fruit is *M. micromalus*, the Small-fruited crab; it is frequently featured in autumn bonsai exhibitions in Japan, when it is quite an impressive sight. Often in the West the particular variety used as bonsai may not be known, as material is acquired from uncertain sources. Those likely to be encountered are Halls crab apple (*M. halliana*), *M. sieboldii*, Toringo crab apple (*M. toringoides*) and *M. cerasifera*.

CARE

Crab apples need to be fed well with a fertilizer that encourages flower production and feeds the fruit. They should not be allowed to produce fruit each year, as this weakens the tree. Every third year they should be rested, and even when allowed to flower and fruit, the fruit should be thinned out considerably after it has set so that the tree is not stressed. Pruning needs to be undertaken by mid-August, otherwise vegetative growth is more likely to occur than flower bud production.

Crab apples attract all sorts of insects and fungal diseases, so they have to be watched carefully and remedial action should be taken as soon as a problem is noticed.

ABOVE Halls crab apple (*Malus halliana*): height 33 cm (13 in); age 17 years. This is a popular species which produces an abundance of flowers and fruits well.

OPPOSITE *Malus halliana*: height 38 cm (15 in); age approximately 30 years. This specimen, shown just coming into flower, is grown in the slanting style and was imported from Japan.

MURRAYA SPP.

DESCRIPTION

Murrayas originate from China, India and Indonesia and are evergreen tropical shrubs that are often used as hedge material in their native countries. Under suitable growing conditions they can achieve heights that give them the status of a small tree. They have glossy leaves which make a dense head of foliage. The flowers are white, bell-shaped and with an aromatic fragrance and they go on to make red berries in the autumn. The bark is fairly smooth and pale-coloured.

Murraya paniculata is the only species that is used for bonsai, and has common names of Satinwood, Orange jasmine and the Cosmetic bark tree. It is a popular bonsai subject in the East – China in particular – and many fine examples fill the pages of bonsai books emanating from that part of the world. In the West it is grown as an indoor bonsai, and specimens encountered of any quality will undoubtedly have been imported as finished bonsai. Murraya bonsai are usually created from cuttings as little material is available for collecting from the wild.

BONSAI STYLES AND PRESENTATION

Murrayas can be grown in a variety of styles, from informal uprights through to cascades. They may be seen occasionally with multi-trunks. The container should be glazed to enhance the presentation of the tree, but it is important for the health of the tree that it is not too shallow. The colour of the pot needs to be chosen carefully to contrast with the colour of the leaves.

SPECIES AND VARIETIES

Murraya paniculata itself has rather large leaves that are feather-like but glossy and leathery. It tends to flower throughout the growing season when kept as a bonsai and

ABOVE *Murraya paniculata:* height 112 cm (44 in); age 80 years. This Chinese bonsai is titled 'Painting of Trees Reaching into the Sky'.

OPPOSITE *Murraya paniculata;* height 88 cm (35 in); age 80 years.

the fruit is shaped like an elongated orange or an olive.

CARE

Murrayas need a very bright, airy, but draught-free position when grown indoors, and should only be given early morning sun. If this is not possible, provide shade for the pot and surface of the compost so that the roots do not get overheated. In winter a heated room is needed. Plenty of warmth is also essential after repotting to encourage new roots to form quickly.

Distilled water should be used to mist the foliage regularly, but watering itself should be kept to a minimum, as it is important not to soak the compost.

New growth needs to be pinched back to a few leaves after the shoots have made six or seven leaves. At other times old leaves should be removed when they turn yellow. When pruning, care should be taken not to remove flower buds.

With so many care provisions to make, Murrayas are not the easiest of subjects for bonsai cultivation.

NANDINA SPP. SACRED BAMBOO, HEAVENLY BAMBOO

DESCRIPTION

Nandinas are sold by ordinary garden centres for normal outside planting in mild regions; they are hardy in all but the coldest areas. In a bonsai pot winter protection is needed.

An evergreen with long, compound leaves, the Nandina's wide spaced leaflets give it a bamboolike appearance. As the tree ages the bark quickly gains a mature-looking quality, and quite young specimens will look much older than they actually are. Nandinas are native to China, India and Japan.

It is a particularly attractive species, for the new leaves are suffused with red before turning green and eventually purplish in the autumn. At most stages of the year it exhibits leaves showing these colours, and among different plants there is considerable variation in the depth and intensity of the colours. The flowers are small and white, sometimes with a hint of yellow. They appear in late summer and can be permitted to go on to form attractive red berries.

BONSAI STYLES AND PRESENTATION

Because of its erect growing habit, Nandina only lends itself to the informal, upright styles. Usually it will have one trunk, or possibly two. The trunk should be heavy and preferably not bulge out at the top where the foliage starts. Such bulging is a result of continual cutting back to that point. More often than not the trunk appears as though a truncheon – not very attractive.

Sometimes several specimens may be placed together to make groups or clumps; they are also used in landscaped arrangements.

Glazed pots are preferred and should be chosen with care to complement the colour of the foliage and the stature of the tree.

SPECIES AND VARIETIES

Nandina domestica is the only species in this genus and it only has a few varieties, such as *N. domestica purpurea.*

CARE

When indoors it should be kept in a bright position. Normal house temperatures and their daily fluctuation will not cause any problem, as this is not really a subtropical species. It is tolerant of light frosts if kept outdoors. In the summer Nandina should be kept outdoors but preferably in light shade. Indoors it should be misted with water daily, and this regime should be continued even when it is outside.

OPPOSITE *Nandina domestica:* height 80 cm (32 in); age estimated at over 500 years. This bonsai has been named 'Gathering of the Dragons' by its Chinese owner.

PICEA SPP. SPRUCE

DESCRIPTION

Spruce are evergreen conifers native to the Northern Hemisphere, where they are mainly found in mountainous regions. The Norway spruce (*P. abies*) is particularly familiar to most people because it is used extensively as a Christmas tree. It is usually thought of as a Fir tree, but it is not.

The foliage of the Spruce is in the form of needles which grow on peglike stumps. Branches form in whorls around the stem, rising upwards slightly. For this reason many find it a difficult subject to make into a bonsai. Cones are quite long and hang from the tips of the branches. The bark is usually dark brown and scaly. The general shape of the tree is conical with a pointed crown, making a stately looking tree when grown as a specimen tree in the open, as well as a bonsai subject.

BONSAI STYLES AND PRESENTATION

Spruce are normally grown as upright trees either formally or in groups. All branches but those at the top of the tree should be horizontal or raked down. Branches should not be left in whorls, but are better raked down from the top of the tall trunk, giving the tree an aged look. To enhance the feeling of age, specimens may have dead-wood effects on them, created by leaving stubs (*jins*) where unwanted branches once were. Bark may be peeled off in a spiral down the trunk to add to the aged effect. Pruning scars should be masked by sticking pieces of the scaly bark over them. Groups may be made up of old trees, although youngsters quickly develop into aged-looking groves or forests.

Pots are usually unglazed in deep colours, and frequently groups will be arranged on slabs of slate or another thin sliver of interesting rock.

ABOVE *Picea abies* 'Little Gem', a dwarf Spruce: height 37 cm (15 in); age 5 years and under training for six months.

TOP Sitka spruce *(Picea sitchensis):* height 30 cm (12 in); age 35 years.

OPPOSITE *Picea mariana* 'Nana', a form of dwarf Spruce: height 10 cm (4in); age 11 years. A *mame* bonsai grown in the slanting style.

BELOW *Picea abies* 'Nidiformis', a dwarf cultivar of the Common or Norway spruce: height 30 cm (12 in); age 10 years and under training.

SPECIES AND VARIETIES

Unless young stock can be acquired, very few of the species and varieties normally encountered are really suitable for bonsai, because most are grafts forming unsightly bulges at the base. One of the favoured dwarf forms is *P. abies albertiana* 'Conica', which is widely available throughout the world and can be made into good bonsai. In Japan the favoured Spruce is Hondo or Yeddo spruce (*P. jezoensis*), which grows extensively on Hondo Island, but is rarely seen in the West.

CARE

When the buds start to break they need to be pinched back to just a few needles by plucking out the end of the extending shoot. Spruce bonsai should be shaded from the midday sun in summer, otherwise the needles go brown as a result of not being able to replace moisture fast enough. Wiring is extensively used for training, but this has to be applied with the utmost care to avoid killing branches, particularly those that are twisted into a new position.

PINUS SPP. PINE

DESCRIPTION

This is the classical bonsai subject in Japan – and the world over, for that matter. Pines make erect growing, stately trees, with powerful and tall trunks that often have bark flaking off in solid plates. Pines are found throughout the Northern Hemisphere, usually in arid and mountainous places. There are many other trees with the word 'pine' in their names that are not Pines at all, and this can make identification and selection confusing at times.

Pine foliage is in the form of needles. Usually these are in bundles of twos or fives, and although some species have bundles of just one, three or even four, these are not often found in bonsai. Some Pines have needles that are very long or that are curved; neither characteristic makes them suitable for bonsai. Colour varies quite considerably.

There is an extensive production industry in Japan for producing cheap but quality embryo Pine bonsai material in a host of styles. If such quality material at low prices were available elsewhere, the interest in bonsai could soar. Unfortunately there are restrictions on importing Pines into Great Britain directly from Japan, but they can be brought in via continental Europe after being quarantined and certified as healthy.

BONSAI STYLES AND PRESENTATION

Pines can be made into all of the bonsai styles. They are most commonly seen as formal trees, and often boring ones at that. They are usually displayed in winter, and before doing so it is not uncommon to discretely wire every branch and twig to get almost every needle into its optimum position.

LEFT Japanese black pine *(Pinus thunbergii):* height 100 cm (39 in); age 30 years.

LEFT Scots pine *(Pinus sylvestris):* height 70 cm (28 in); age 40 years. This example has been created in the literati style with a jinned apex.

LEFT A Japanese white pine *(Pinus parviflora, also known as P. pentaphylla)* is shown on display at a Japanese bonsai exhibition in Osaka.

ABOVE Japanese white pine *(Pinus parviflora):* height 84 cm (33 in); age 30 years. This is an impressive example and grown in the informal upright style.

Sometimes Pines may be seen on display after having had their needles reduced in size with shears, but this distracts from the beauty of the tree because the cut ends turn brown. Really good specimens will have noticeably thick and ridged bark.

Impressive Pine bonsai needs to be planted in deep pots commensurate with their stature, and deep, earthy colours are usually used. White pines, which are lighter in appearance, may be housed in lightly glazed and less powerful-looking pots.

SPECIES AND VARIETIES

There are three species extensively used for Pine bonsai in Japan. These are the Japanese black pine (*P. thunbergii*), Japanese red pine (*P. densiflora*) and Japanese white pine (*P. parviflora*). The native two-needled Scots or Scotch pine (*P. sylvestris*) and its dwarf forms, 'Nana', 'Beuvronensis' and 'Watereri'

are extensively used as alternatives to the Japanese black. The dwarf Mountain or Swiss pine (*P. mugo*) is also very popular and quite ideal for bonsai. Much of it is propagated for garden use, so it is readily and cheaply available.

CARE

Pines only need infrequent repotting. When they are very old – well over 100 – repotting may need to be done only every 10 to 15 years. Meticulous care needs to be paid to keeping needles short by removing the buds, and to shortening the candles. Timing is critical here and more has been written on this subject than any other in bonsai.

Pines should be kept on the dry side for most of the year, and at the time of spring growth water needs to be withheld to help keep needles short. They should be planted in very well-draining soil.

LEFT Japanese white pine *(Pinus parviflora):* height 70 cm (28 in); age 30 years. This bonsai is seemingly precariously clasped to the rock.

PODOCARPOS SPP.

DESCRIPTION

This is a large genus of shrubs and trees that much resemble the *Taxus* species (Yews), and Podocarpos are often referred to generally as Yellow woods or Southern yews. They emanate from the Far East and thus prefer warmer temperatures, and even tropical conditions in some cases, in which to survive.

Like the Yews they are evergreen and the foliage at first glance is not too dissimilar, but the general disposition of the tree is to make branches that grow horizontally in contrast to the upright growth in Yews. Inspection of the back of the needle-type leaf shows prominent white bands of breathing pores known as stomata.

In the Far East, particularly Hong Kong, Podocarpos in the form of *P. macrophyllus* is a highly prized subject for bonsai because it is slow-growing and it takes a long time to create a top quality specimen. In the West, Podocarpos are usually considered an indoor bonsai subject rather than one for outdoors.

BONSAI STYLES
AND PRESENTATION

Podocarpos can be trained into a variety of bonsai styles, but informal treatments are best, including split trunks, and the display of a considerable amount of dead wood (driftwood) in the arrangement. Cascade styles, small groups and even forest plantings are also seen. In the West, natural looking styles are likely to be encountered, in comparison to the artificially contrived arrangements that abound in the East.

SPECIES AND VARIETIES

The favoured subject for bonsai use is *P. macrophyllus*, which has several common names to add to its confusion – Kusamakia, or just Maki, Buddhist pine, Chinese yew and Swallow's tongue pine. Other species likely to be used in the West are the dwarf forms *P. nivalis* and *P. alpinus* which have smaller and less coarse foliage.

CARE

Most Podocarpos will need some form of winter protection. However, the environmental conditions that any particular species requires can vary considerably, so guidance should be taken from the supplier if you acquire one as a finished bonsai. New growth should be pruned with scissors rather than with the fingers. General tidying of trees can be undertaken at any time of the year, as this species can be clipped with impunity just as Yews can.

Repotting of Podocarpos should only be undertaken infrequently, and even then only a small portion of the root should be removed. When indoors, frequent misting is needed and in summer a long spell outdoors will help to ensure the continued health of the tree.

ABOVE

*Podocarpos macrophyllus
maki:* height 50 cm (18 in);
age 60 years.

PRUNUS SPP.

DESCRIPTION

This genus contains many distinctly different species in terms of their general appearance, flowers and fruit. In the main they make small-sized trees, although some are nothing more than quite small shrubs. The bark is usually distinctive, sometimes deep-coloured and glossy with horizontal bands of breathing cells known as lenticels. Leaves are elliptical, usually deciduous, and vary from extra large in size to being delightfully small. Most species will be encountered as ornamentals growing in gardens, although Sloe (*P. spinosa*), a spined species, grows extensively in old hedges, when its small white flowers come to the fore in early spring.

In the main the flowers are extremely showy, varying from pure white through to all shades of pinks and reds. Some are small, and small-flowered species are more highly prized as bonsai than the double-flowered cultivars. The *Prunus* species are renowned for their fruit – cherries, plums, damsons, peaches, sloes and apricots. As bonsai they are essentially grown for their flowers.

Extensively used for bonsai, trees of quality will be specimens collected from the wild or grubbed up out of gardens when past their prime as a garden tree.

BONSAI STYLES AND PRESENTATION

Members of this genus are invariably grown in informal styles, and are displayed in spring when in full flower. Many of the really impressive Cherry or Apricot bonsai often have much of the heart wood of the trunk eaten away, to leave just an interesting fretwork of old wood.

Where larger-flowered cultivars are used as bonsai subjects, the tree should also be proportionally large in size. Glazed pots will invariably be used.

TOP Prunus species: height 55 cm (22 in). A flowering Cherry on display in a private collection in Japan.

ABOVE Prunus species – a weeping-type Cherry; height 30 cm (12 in); age approximately 15 years.

SPECIES AND VARIETIES

Most of the ornamental Cherries and other members of this genus have their origins in Japan. Fuji cherry (*P. incisa*) is grown for its small white flowers. The Bush cherries (*P. tomentosa* and *P. sinensis*) have pink or white pompom-like flowers and are small-leaved and thus ideal for bonsai use. Higan cherry or Rosebud cherry (*P. subhirtella*) is favoured in the West and can flower from late autumn onward.

Japanese apricot (*P. mume*), has rich-coloured but large flowers, and sometimes displays different colours on the same tree through grafting. The Peach (*P. persica*) has larger flowers than most other members of this genus, and when used for bonsai lacks delicacy in comparison with other species.

There are innumerable cultivars to be found in this genus, too numerous to mention, and the large-flowered ones should be avoided for bonsai.

CULTIVATION

All members of the genus are quite easy to cultivate. After flowering they need to be deadheaded. Little pruning is usually necessary, but deep pruning is sometimes needed to regenerate flowering shoots. If cherries require shaping, copper wire must not be used. Feeding should be with a view to producing flowers when the basic design of the tree has been created. A fertilizer high in potassium should be used during the second half of the year.

RIGHT *Prunus pissardii* — a species of flowering Cherry: height 30 cm (12 in); age 8 years.

PUNICA SPP. POMEGRANATE

DESCRIPTION

Pomegranate is native to Asia and the Mediterranean area. At best pomegranates only make small, densely twigged deciduous trees with narrow, alternate leaves. The leaves fall in the autumn, unless the tree is grown exclusively indoors; then growth is usually continuous. The dwarf form of the Pomegranate has better foliage; it is smaller leaved and tinged with reds and golds.

The intense, red-coloured flowers form at the end of new shoots from midsummer onwards. These flowers go on to make the familiar pomegranate fruit. The bark is light in colour, and in a mature tree takes on an interesting quality and distinctive pattern.

BONSAI STYLES AND PRESENTATION

Good specimens are few and far between in the West, as few quality trees have been exported from Japan. Often they are made with what seems to be a twisted trunk; this results from plaiting young trees together or winding one around a piece of dead material. In the latter case the centre material rots away in the course of time, leaving a hollow trunk behind. Many quality Pomegranate bonsai show the telltale signs of such techniques. Other Pomegranate bonsai come from old specimens that have been reduced severely in size to almost nothing, or from an air-layer taken from an old bonsai tree.

Pomegranate is ideal for making into small bonsai, but if allowed to flower will look a mess. A large specimen is preferable because it will be in proportion to the rather large flowers which form at the end of the new growth. New growth must be allowed to extend; pruning and pinching it back to retain the overall shape of the tree will mean a loss of the flower buds.

Pomegranates are usually housed in glazed pots that are sometimes quite ornate. Light blue is a popular colour.

SPECIES AND VARIETIES

P. granatum, either in its normal or dwarf form, is the species used for bonsai.

CARE

In mild and temperate areas, Pomegranates are best kept outdoors in the summer. They should be given half shade and fed well with an appropriate fertilizer to encourage flowering. The foliage should be constantly thinned out, with a few shoots allowed to extend to carry the odd flower. If fruit forms it should not be allowed to grow to full size, as this will sap the tree of its energy. In the autumn it is best to overwinter it in a cool place so that it can go into dormancy and rest for a while.

LEFT *Punica granatum flavesens:* height 50 cm (20 in); age 35 years. A Chinese specimen, this tree has been named 'Dark Roaming Dragon Hunting for Pearls'.

RIGHT *Punica granatum,* a species of Pomegranate: height 175cm (69in); age 100 years. The unusual height of this specimen allows the tree to carry fruit.

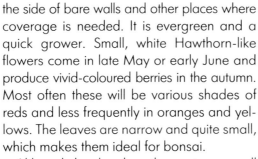

PYRACANTHA SPP. FIRETHORN

DESCRIPTION

This shrub is commonly found growing up the side of bare walls and other places where coverage is needed. It is evergreen and a quick grower. Small, white Hawthorn-like flowers come in late May or early June and produce vivid-coloured berries in the autumn. Most often these will be various shades of reds and less frequently in oranges and yellows. The leaves are narrow and quite small, which makes them ideal for bonsai.

Although hardy when the roots are well down in the ground, Pyracanthas are easily destroyed by frosts when planted in shallow pots. For this reason some consider them indoor bonsai.

BONSAI STYLES
AND PRESENTATION

Pyracantha are at their best when in flower or when the berries have come into full colour. All flowers and berries should be in perfect condition when on show. The trunk of the tree should be powerful and visible, and when on display the flowers and fruit should not be uniformly distributed over the tree.

Single specimens through to multitree plantings may well be seen, and the trunks may be upright, slanted, horizontal or fully cascading. Most often they will be upright, and tightly clothed with foliage rather than having a light and open structure. No dead leaves should be present when in flower. Old leaves are replaced, and they go yellow before dropping over a period of several months each spring. Any leaves will have to be picked off by hand before the tree is put on show.

They look best when planted in light-coloured, glazed pots that are either chosen to complement the colour of the flowers or berries, whichever is considered to be the more important show aspect. Deep but not garish blues are also ideal.

SPECIES AND VARIETIES

There are only a comparatively few species of Pyracantha. The one most likely to be seen is *P. angustifolia*, which is narrow-leaved and freely flowering and fruiting.

CARE

Pyracanthas are a very thirsty species and need to be well watered, even when little growth is taking place. They need to be fed well, too, and every third year they should be rested by removing all of the flowers as they form; constant flowering when in a pot can result in a tree that is overstressed.

Pyracanthas need to be overwintered in a frost-free place, such as a cold frame, or brought inside to an unheated room. Feeding should be with a view to flower and fruit production, rather than for vegetative growth. Berries are usually removed by the end of the year, and prior to that netting may be necessary to protect the fruit from birds, especially if you wish to show your bonsai late in the season.

BELOW *Pyracantha crenulata:* height 162 cm (64 in); age 45 years. This is a very light and delicate looking bonsai in the literati style.

OPPOSITE *Pyracantha angustifolia* 'Orange Charmer': height 19 cm (7 in); spread 40 cm (16 in); age 8 years. This bonsai is in the horizontal or semi-cascading style and was developed from ordinary garden centre stock.

PYRUS SPP. PEAR

DESCRIPTION

The Pear is an underrated, small- to medium-sized deciduous tree that is little used for bonsai, either in the West nor in Japan. Depending on the species and variety, it has leaves that vary in size from quite small to large and come in various shades of green, ranging from dull green to bright, fresh-coloured green. The leaves are alternate on the shoot, and autumn colour is usually poor. The leaves of some Pears are rather apple-shaped, being more round than long; this can cause confusion when determining whether young stock is Apple or Pear.

Flowers develop on short spurs and usually appear in late March a month or so before those of Crab apples. They are white and strongly scented with crimson centres. The bark is rough and deeply furrowed, and the general growing habit of the tree is character-ized by a few erect growing branches dotted with thorns.

BONSAI STYLES
AND PRESENTATION

When a Pear bonsai is displayed in flower, one can generally assume that the tree is 20 or more years old since Pears take a long time to reach flowering maturity. Really aged specimens are likely to be the remnants of old orchard trees or are trees that were prop-agated by air-layering already flowering trees. Sometimes grafts are used but in good bonsai there should be no noticeable bulge at the graft union.

Pears are developed in informal styles, from uprights through to cascades. Cascades need to be designed with great care so that arrangments do not look too stiff and stilted. Small clumps and groups can often be seen as well.

The small-leaved species are ideal for making into small- to medium-sized bonsai,

especially when a small and bright-leaved subject is used. Leaves must be in perfect condition when the tree is on show, and there must be no signs of fungal attack.

Shallow glazed pots are generally used to enhance the lightness and openness of the Pear's structure. Pale colours including whites and creams look good.

SPECIES AND VARIETIES

The species *P. simonii* is used in Japan, but this is not usually found in the West. The Willow-leaved pear (*P. salicifolia*) can make an interesting tree in the weeping style, and the Sand pear (*P. sinensis*) is particularly suited to being made into a bonsai.

CARE

Pears are attacked by a fungus which turns the leaves a deep ebony colour. Once it starts to show in midsummer, remedial spraying with a fungicide is needed, and affected leaves should be removed and destroyed. Feeding should be carried out with the aim of producing flower buds, and after flowering is over the tree should be deadheaded so as not to let fruit form.

Pears can be quite touchy after repotting, and when undertaken it is customary to leave most of the roots undisturbed. Repotting in autumn rather than in the spring should be the norm.

OPPOSITE Pyrus
species, pear: height 63 cm
(25 in); age 13 years.
Grown from seed in the
twin-trunk style.

QUERCUS SPP. OAK

DESCRIPTION

Oak is a large genus that can be found throughout the Northern Hemisphere and even in the tropics. As yet it has not gained a reputation as a good subject for bonsai, and it appears to be little used even in Japan. The many species range from deciduous trees usually with quite large leaves, to a few evergreens and a number of crossbred species. Mature Oaks have dark grey, fissured bark. The leaves tend to grow in tufts at the end of the twigs rather than evenly spread around the shoots; this makes them difficult to work with as bonsai. They are also not well favoured because they attract so many bugs and are attacked by a whole range of fungal diseases.

BONSAI STYLES AND PRESENTATION

Oaks make large, impressive trees in their natural state, and this grand stature really needs to be encapsulated into a bonsai Oak, whether it be deciduous or evergreen. It should be fairly upright and have a slightly informal look to it. There are very few good Oak bonsai, let alone ones of real quality. Most that are seen in the West have been collected from open fields, severely reduced, and a year later presented for show. They are far from convincing, lacking style, elegance and, most importantly, compactness. They look like just what they are – scrubby trees chopped back. No doubt with the passage of time good-quality Oaks will be produced in the West.

Foliage must be small, compact and, most importantly, perfectly clean and healthy when on display. Leaves must not have been reduced by cutting them down in size to the same shape with scissors.

Pots are usually glazed and in light and textured, earthy colours. For the health of the tree they need to be a little deeper than most bonsai pots.

SPECIES AND VARIETIES

There is a considerable number of species of Oak, most of which are not at all suited for bonsai use because of the size of the leaves and their arrangement on the shoots. English or Truffle oak (*Q. robur*) and Sessile or Durmast oak (*Q. petraea*) will be most frequently seen, as will the fast-growing Turkey oak (*Q. cerris*). The Japanese use the Daimyo oak (*Q. dentata*) which has leaves up to 30cm (1ft) long.

CARE

Because of its tendency to attract all kinds of diseases, Oak is a demanding tree when grown as a bonsai. It does not respond well to pruning techniques to reduce leaf size. Complete defoliation often results in the leaves coming back even larger. Infrequent repotting helps, as does the removal of all terminal buds just before leaf break.

LEFT English or Truffle
oak *(Quercus robur):* height
83 cm (33 in); age
50 years. This oak bonsai is
of exceptional quality by
Western *and* Eastern
standards.

RHODODENDRON SPP. AZALEA, RHODODENDRON

DESCRIPTION

For practical bonsai purposes Azaleas and Rhododendrons are grouped together even though experts disagree as to whether they are one or two distinct species. They consist of a genus of shrubs renowned for the quality and variety of their flowers. They are currently in vogue as bonsai, particularly in Japan. Many excellent bonsai specimens were created in Japan in the 1920s when the small-leaved Azaleas were particularly popular there. Leaves can be quite small in size depending on the species, or very large as is usually the case with Rhododendrons. The smaller-leaved Azaleas are usually used for bonsai, and as semievergreen rather than deciduous shrubs. The leaves are deep green and glossy, which enhances the brilliance of the flowers.

As a genus they are exclusively confined to the Northern Hemisphere, and most species come from mountainous regions in China and Tibet.

BONSAI STYLES AND PRESENTATION

Azaleas are mainly only of interest when in flower, but some of the Rhododendrons that have been field grown and have acquired large and impressive trunks may be seen on display from time to time when out of flower. When in flower the specimen can be covered entirely with them, completely obliterating the foliage. Flower buds break out over a period of time, and it is not until most are out that the tree looks neat and presentable. This is because the bells of the flowers tend to point in a number of directions, giving an unkempt appearance. Azaleas are best shown with pockets of bright fresh greenery and some areas of the tree completely dis-budded, so as to give some relief from the mass of flowers.

ABOVE A variety of Satzuki azalea *(Rhododendron lateritium komei)* height 37 cm (15 in); age approximately 18 years. A detail of the flowers is shown opposite.

BELOW Rhododendron 'Blue Tit' is a popular small-flowered Rhododendron: height 38 cm (15 in); age 30 years.

The best-quality Azalea bonsai will have informal treelike shapes, but the majority are likely to be seen in a vast variety of styles and presentations. Mainly they will be seen with thin trunks, and these should be without pruning scars. Imported specimens will often be grown with a series of repeated S bends up the length of the trunk, a popular commercially produced style until recently. Coloured glazed pots are the norm.

SPECIES AND VARIETIES

Azaleas and Rhododendrons are an extremely large genus in terms of both the species but particularly the varieties. The Satzuki azalea (*Rhododendron lateritium*, also called *R. indicum* in some books) produces many sports with such exotic names as Hanna No Tsukasa and Hanafubuki. The Kurume azalea (*R. obtusum*) is used extensively in the West, and of the Rhododendrons proper, the small-flowered shrubby *R. impeditum* is now being recommended, and the variation in its flowers is almost infinite. In Japan there are two monthly bonsai magazines devoted just to Satzuki azaleas.

Many of the species in this genus, and particularly the Rhododendrons, have flowers that are too large for use as bonsai. The larger the flower, the larger the structure has to be and the fewer the number of flowers.

CARE

Azaleas and Rhododendrons vary enormously in hardiness when grown as ornamentals, but when under bonsai conditions they are not too hardy and winter protection is needed. If frosts do cut the leaves back, the tree will regenerate them in due course. Sometimes all of the branches are removed deliberately, such as when a restructure of the tree is needed, and deep pruning always results in prolific budding down the stems and branches by the end of the growing season.

They are very fussy about their growing conditions and need a lime-free soil. Hard water has to be avoided; either rain or distilled water should be used instead.

SAGERETIA SPP.

DESCRIPTION

Sageretias are small shrubs that come from central and southern Asia and are grown extensively as bonsai in China. Some of them have thorns. Branches are stiff and slender, and the bark is scaly, peeling off in flakes rather like the bark of Plane trees and Trident maples. The leaves are small, shiny and evergreen, and when young have a pinkish tinge to them. The flowers are white with a hint of green and develop in the leaf axils of the new shoots. They are small and insignificant and go on to make small blue berries.

Many good specimens are currently being imported. Most need considerable work to develop them to their full potential. Those coming from China are said to be specimens collected from the wild.

BONSAI STYLES
AND PRESENTATION

Sageretias usually have a definite masculine appearance to them. Those imported are almost invariably styled in a Chinese way, with a stiff main stem, usually with little taper and only clothed with foliage at a few places. They are a species that can be grown in a number of different styles so long as they are of an informal character. Those bonsai with softer, rounder shapes are more likely to have been created as a bonsai by man, rather than having been developed from material collected from the wild.

BELOW *Sageretia theezans:* spread 50 cm (20 in); age 15 years – a delightfully delicate cascade in a hand-crafted pot.

Imported trees are usually in Chinese pots that are crude and heavy in appearance, with a uniform and deep-coloured glaze that is not to Western taste. Ideally they should be repotted into a more appropriate container, that is usually shallower, in order to enhance presentation. Lighter colours help to show the foliage off to its best.

SPECIES AND VARIETIES

The species *S. theezans*, for which there appears to be no common name, is almost invariably used as bonsai.

CARE

Sageretia needs plenty of light, and can be kept outdoors from late spring until the end of summer. It needs moderate temperatures all the year round, and even indoors in the winter care should be taken to keep it sufficiently warm. Humidity should be kept high, either by daily misting or by standing the potted specimen on a tray filled with gravel and water. To encourage flowering growth needs to be left unchecked. Oversized leaves can be removed by hand if they spoil the look of the tree.

RIGHT *Sageretia theezans,* also known as *S. thea:* height 100 cm (39 in); age 100 years.

SALIX SPP. WILLOW

DESCRIPTION

The Weeping willow (*S. babylonia*) is the most commonly encountered member of this quite extensive genus. In addition to those few species that make handsome deciduous trees, there are many naturally shrubby species to be found that most people would not recognize as a Willow.

Leaf break is normally very early, and in many, but not all, of the species it follows after the catkins have come out. The buds on many of the ornamental Willows look as though they are dead until they start to break open and allow the emergence of the white or pale yellow catkins.

Foliage is usually light green. The shoots, which are often highly coloured, grow very quickly in some species and carry the leaves alternately, in a spreading rather than compact arrangement. Many of the stems are red, which gives the tree extra appeal when Willows are displayed just after the catkins have come out.

BONSAI STYLES
AND PRESENTATION

Willow only has a short period of glory each year. This is in the spring when the foliage is fresh. It quickly turns very mangy after maturing and only rarely would the tree be displayed again until the following spring. Those species and varieties that are prolific in making catkins can be enjoyed before leaf break, but to prevent the catkins going mushy, the tree is best kept out of rain until flowering is over.

The dwarf forms are ideal subjects for bonsai and Willows should have thick and heavy trunks whether the tree is very small or large. Those that reach tree size in Nature need to be developed to display the fresh shoots in a cascading manner. The styles will always be informal.

ABOVE Crack willow *(Salix fragilis):* height 20 cm (8 in). This award-winning bonsai has been under training for twelve years and was originally created from an extra large cutting.

SPECIES AND VARIETIES

The White willow (*S. alba*) and the Weeping willow (*S. babylonica*) are the best species for larger-sized bonsai. As far as the dwarf and shrubby ornamental species are concerned, it is a matter of using what you can find; similarly so with the hybrids, which may be found occasionally.

CARE

Willows are a very thirsty species of tree and quite happy to have their feet in water. All Willows are therefore best stood in a bowl of water through the summer. Root growth is so vigorous that repotting twice a year is not uncommon. Many growers keep their Willow bonsai in the open ground for most of the year, digging it up in early spring so that it can be put into its bonsai pot and its fresh foliage enjoyed at its best. Afterwards, they return the tree to the ground until the following spring.

Heavy pruning must be done each year to keep foliage compact and close to the trunk, particularly in the dwarf forms. To produce weeping branches much care and expertise is needed, for when growing as a bonsai, weeping stems do not form naturally but have to be encouraged by judicious pruning and the use of wire or weights.

RIGHT A species of Salix (Willow): height 61 cm (24 in); age 40 years.

LEFT Goat willow *(Salix caprea);* when this specimen was collected from the wild, the top had already rotted away.

SEQUOIA SEMPERVIRENS CALIFORNIA REDWOOD
SEQUOIADENDRON GIGANTEUM WELLINGTONIA

DESCRIPTION

Both the California redwood (*Sequoia sempervirens*) and the Wellingtonia (*Sequoiadendron giganteum*) seem unlikely species to be used for bonsai, as they make the tallest trees in the world, achieving heights of between 90 to 113 metres (300–370 ft). Using them for bonsai does, therefore, prove that no tree species is beyond possibility. Although these trees are only found on the Pacific Coast of the United States, both species, particularly the Wellingtonia, are becoming increasingly popular in the West as bonsai subjects due to their very rapid growth rate – quite impressive bonsai can be created in just a few years.

Both of these species have red, thick spongy bark that peels off in long strips, and make exceptional buttressing in the lower part of the trunk to support the massive height of the tree. The two species can be distinguished by the leaves and the bark. The leaves of the Wellingtonia, when crushed, give off an unpleasant odour, and the bark is deeply fluted as against fissured in the California redwood. The leaves of the Wellingtonia are also scale-like whereas in the California redwood they are clearly differentiated resembling Yews and Hemlocks.

BONSAI STYLES AND PRESENTATION

Both species can readily be made into bonsai that truly resemble the stature and general appearance of the tree when found growing naturally. However, as bonsai subjects, they should only be created in the upright style, preferably in a formal arrangement with all branches sweeping down to emulate a mature appearance. They also lend themselves to having their trunks split, again to indicate age. Arrangements of two or a few trees together make very effective bonsai.

These are subjects that are best displayed in spring when showing new growth, as this gives the tree an extra sparkle. Deeper rather than shallower pots are needed.

SPECIES AND VARIETIES

The Sequoia and Sequoiadendron both have just the one species. Each has a few cultivars and a small form that may well be sought out for bonsai use: *Sequoia sempervirens* 'Prostata', also called 'Nana Pendula' and *Sequoiadendron giganteum* 'Pygmaeum'.

CARE

Both need plenty of water and are easy to cultivate provided regular attention is paid to keeping growth under control. They are best given some shade in the height of summer, particularly if a very free-draining compost is used. In winter frost protection is needed.

LEFT The Wellingtonia
*(Sequoiadendron
giganteum):* height 55 cm
(22 in); age 19 years;
produced from ordinary
garden centre container-
grown stock.

SERISSA FOETIDA TREE OF A THOUSAND STARS

DESCRIPTION

Serissa foetida is a favoured species for indoor bonsai in the West, and as an outdoor bonsai in China, Japan and Southeast Asia, where it has its origins. It is an evergreen shrub with small, bright green, oval leaves. In late spring small white flowers cover the tree, and flowering continues for several months. It sometimes flowers out of season, as a consequence of the conditions under which it is being kept.

It naturally makes many branches, and this makes shaping easy when grown as a bonsai. The natural colour of the trunk is grey, and the bark roughens with age, turning to white in old specimens.

BONSAI STYLES AND PRESENTATION

Serissa can be made into almost all of the bonsai styles, but is more effective when in an informal arrangement. Its trunk is naturally on the slim side, so a bonsai with a fat trunk will be indicative of considerable age. When on display no yellow leaves should be left on, nor should there be any sucker growth at the base.

Deep-coloured glazed pots are ideal for this species. These can also be highly decorated, and the depth should be commensurate with the stature of the trunk.

SPECIES AND VARIETIES

S. foetida is also known as *S. japonica*, and it is the main species used for Serissa bonsai. *Foetida* means foul-smelling, and the word is aptly applied, as the bark and roots have a most unpleasant smell when crushed or cut. Usually *S. foetida* will be seen in the single-flowered variety, but there is a double-flowered form as well. There are also golden and ivory-green variegated forms that are sometimes used.

CARE

Being a subtropical species, *S. foetida* is kept indoors for most of the year, where it likes a bright but not too sunny position. If summers are warm both night and day it can – and should – be kept outdoors then in a slightly shaded place.

Leaf drop is due to being kept in too cool a place or somewhere where light conditions are wrong. Sudden changes in the growing environment can also cause leaf drop, but new foliage soon returns.

Dead flower heads should be removed daily to prolong the flowering period. Frequent misting with warm water is appreciated, but do not use harsh tap water that can leave a lime deposit on the leaves and spoil the appearance of the tree. Distilled water should be used instead.

ABOVE Tree of a
thousand stars *(Serissa
foetida):* height 48 cm
(19 in); age 15 years.
This specimen has been
grown on sedimentary
sandstone in a Chinese-
styled arrangement.

TAMARIX SPP. TAMARISK

DESCRIPTION

Tamarisks are an ideal subject to use to produce a light and delicate looking bonsai with slender and graceful branches. The foliage is plume-like and of a light-green colour. In mid spring they produce light-pink flowers that give the tree the quality of an impressionistic watercolour.

They only make specimens of shrub-sized proportions unless grown under very favourable conditions and are commonly found growing in coastal areas where they seem to thrive on the sea breezes. Inland they appreciate a sunny position.

BONSAI STYLES AND PRESENTATION

Tamarisk bonsai will invariably be found trained into an informal style, and usually with a shape not conforming to the standard shapes into which other species are melded when created as bonsai. Better bonsai specimens will usually have been created from unwanted material taken out of the garden or collected from the wild. Trunks may well be split down to create an aged appearance and parts of the trunk hollowed out where unwanted major stems have been removed.

Whatever the chosen style, the foliage must look graceful; arching branches will give the appearance of a weeping style. The windsept style is also ideal for this species.

Pots should be shallow and glazed, and not formal in appearance, maybe with some ornamentation on the lipping and footings of the pot. Deeper rather than lighter colours will be preferable to contrast with the light-coloured foliage.

SPECIES AND VARIETIES

Tamarisks belong to a genus with only a few species and even fewer varieties and cultivars. Common species are *T. juniperiana* and *T. pentandra*. The latter has a cultivar – 'Rubra' – that has deep red flowers.

CARE

Tamarisks are not easy to cultivate successfully as bonsai. They have a disconcerting habit of simply dying for no known reason. Pruning has to be undertaken at the correct time for the species, as some Tamarisks flower on old wood while others do so on the growth made earlier the same year. In the former case pruning has to be undertaken immediately after flowering and no later, else the flower buds for the following year will be removed. Tamarisks generally require full sunlight.

OPPOSITE *Tamarix chinensis:* height 35 cm (14 in); age 30 years; in a weeping-foliage styled bonsai.

TAXODIUM DISTICHUM SWAMP, BALD CYPRESS

DESCRIPTION

Swamp cypress is not a true cypress. It is a large and powerful deciduous tree that, when growing in its natural habitat usually has its 'feet' in water, or in water-logged soil. It buttresses far more impressively than most other trees, and when growing in water sends up woody protruberances, called knees, from the ground several feet away from the main stem. These knees are thought to provide air for the roots, for when Swamp cypress grows in dry conditions knees do not form.

The translation of the Japanese name for this tree is the Feather-falling pine, an apt name for a tree with featherlike leaves in the form of long sprays of light-green flat needles. The foliage resembles that of the Dawn redwood (*Metasequoia glyptostroboides*), but instead of being alternate on the shoot, the leaves are slightly offset from one another. In the autumn the foliage turns brown before dropping, often persisting on the tree for a long time afterwards. The bark is reddish-brown and thin, peeling off in long strips.

There are some handsome specimens growing in parks in Europe, but as a bonsai it is most likely to be seen and collected in the United States, where it grows in the Florida swamps.

BONSAI STYLES AND PRESENTATION

This species can make impressive bonsai, particularly if older material with a powerful buttress and some character in the lower trunk can be acquired. They can be made into formal uprights, as well as all the upright in-formal styles. When they have a powerful trunk they can be made into trees containing just a little foliage, to accentuate the feeling of maturity.

The structure of a Swamp cypress bonsai should be very simple and uncomplicated,

with very few branches. Older specimens may carry a lot of deadwood effects on the trunk, and they could even be partially hollowed out. Pruning scars should be masked with strips of the bark stuck over them.

SPECIES AND VARIETIES

Taxodiums only have a few species, and there are even fewer varieties. The Pond cypress (*T. ascendens*) and Mexican or Montezuma cypress (*T. mucronatum*) is rarely seen in Europe, although both are more common in the United States.

CARE

Even though when in the wild Swamp cypress often grows with its 'feet' in water, when grown as a bonsai it should be watered as any other tree. Keeping the pot in a bowl of water does not help to make knees form; knees are not likely to form under any bonsai conditions. Unlike most other bonsai, which prefer alkaline soil, Swamp cypress does best in acidic soil.

Swamp cypress is not an easy subject to keep compact, hence the need for a simple structure. If hard pruning is not done after leaf fall they become very straggly. When new growth starts the many buds forming on the stem or in unwanted places on the branches should be rubbed off periodically.

RIGHT *Taxodium distichum:* this example has very unusual bends in the trunk.

LEFT Bald or Swamp
cypress *(Taxodium
distichum):* age
approximately 80 years;
note the good buttressing of
the roots.

TAXUS SPP. YEW

DESCRIPTION

Although in the West there are only a few good bonsai specimens, Yews are one of the needle evergreens that make high-quality bonsai. The needles are arranged spirally around the shoot and appear as though in two flattened ranks. Young trees at first grow erect, but with age tend to spread. Trunks are usually on the slim side, and heavy and impressive trunks on old trees are thought to be not one trunk but a fusion of several. The bark is of a rich purple-red colour and scaly, peeling off in strips. Yews are only likely to be confused with Hemlocks, which have a similar foliage arrangement.

BONSAI STYLES AND PRESENTATION

Yews can be put on display almost any time of the year, but they are not likely to be seen when in flower because they shed an enormous amount of fine, creamy white pollen. They are at their best when the new flush of growth comes in the spring; any dead leaves remaining from past seasons should have been removed. In the autumn a fine specimen can be expected to carry at least a few red, fleshy cones.

Older specimens of Yew that have been collected from the wild are likely to show a considerable amount of dead wood, which gives them a very aged appearance. All but young bonsai should appear rugged, as though they have suffered the ravages of time. Yews with thick trunks are likely to have been collected from the wild, for under bonsai cultivation the trunks do not thicken very well. No man-made scars should be seen on the trunk, other than those created for effect; pruning cuts should be masked by covering them with strips of bark taken from other parts of the tree. Yews are sometimes grown in small groups of young trees.

ABOVE Common or English yew *(Taxus baccata)*: height 26 cm (10 in); age 14 years. This bonsai was collected as a one-year-old seedling.

OPPOSITE *Taxus baccata:* height 28 cm (11 in); age 12 years; grown in the 'grump' (group-on-a hump style) from seed.

Pots are likely to be unglazed and fairly plain. A pot in the shape of a crescent is sometimes used for a windswept style tree.

SPECIES AND VARIETIES

There are only a few species of Yew. In the West the Common or English yew (*T. baccata*) is used, while the Japanese use the very similar Japanese yew (*T. cuspidata*). There a few coloured varieties which are not very hardy and do not grow well in a bonsai pot. The very erect growing species and varieties are very seldom made into bonsai.

CARE

Yews are quite easy to maintain as bonsai. The ends of new growth need to be plucked out to maintain the general shape. They are quite happy in heavy shade and maintain their colour well. For fruit to be produced, a female tree is needed, and it has to be pollinated either by a nearby male bonsai or by a tree growing in the garden. Yews grown from seed are usually males.

LEFT *Taxus baccata:* extent 50 cm (20 in) from apex to tip of tail; age 15 years. Grown as a cascade, this Yew bonsai is still in the early stages of development.

TSUGA SPP. HEMLOCK

DESCRIPTION

Hemlocks are likely to be seen more frequently as a bonsai than are Firs, which they resemble. Although they look similar, Hemlocks are more delicately foliaged and have smaller leaves. In their natural habitat they achieve heights of well over 30 m (100 ft). The bark is cinnamon-red and becomes deeply furrowed with age. The branches naturally take on a drooping habit. The cones are small and pale brown when mature; after dropping their seed they remain on the tree for quite a long time.

BONSAI STYLES AND PRESENTATION

Hemlocks are ideal for both formal and informal style trees. Those made from a species rather than a dwarf variety are likely to be more stately in appearance. In a formal style tree branches should droop, which is a general sign of age in conifers. Erect growing branches typify youth. Sometimes Hemlocks may be seen with branches growing upwards and then turning over at the ends, giving a weeping effect.

Hemlocks also lend themselves to being grown in groups planted in shallow trays. Sometimes they may be grown in what is called the raft style; the trunk is laid horizontal, allowed to root, and what were previously branches become a series of trunks

SPECIES AND VARIETIES

Hemlocks are found throughout the whole of the Northern Hemisphere. The Eastern or Canadian hemlock (*T. canadensis*) is available in a range of varieties, most of which are shrubby and very appealing as bonsai. Dwarf forms are more likely to be used for bonsai as they are often available in garden centres in large sizes, thus lending themselves to being converted into an interesting bonsai.

Frequently encountered is the culivar *T. canadensis* 'Jedoloh', which has a common name of Bird's nest tree because of its habit of spreading and forming a depression in the crown that resembles a bird's nest. The Western hemlock (*T. heterophylla*) is not readily available in ordinary garden centres and consequently is little used for bonsai. This is only because it is a forest tree and has to be obtained from specialist nurseries. In Japan Japanese hemlock (*T. diversifolia*) is mainly used.

CARE

Hemlocks grow slowly, almost imperceptibly. As new growth is more or less the same colour as the old foliage, extension growth tends to go unnoticed, and the tree gradually gets out of shape. It then needs to be pruned back hard at the end of the year so that the foliage pads remain compact and die-back is minimalized. Shade is usually recommended for the summer. Hemlocks are not at all fussy about their growing conditions, and apart from the need to pinch back and thin out the foliage they take care of themselves.

FOLLOWING PAGE

Tsuga canadensis 'Jedoloh':
height 37 cm (15 in); age
approximately 20 years;
developed into a bonsai
from ordinary garden
centre stock.

ULMUS SPP. ELM

DESCRIPTION

Elms make stately trees, and until the advent of Dutch elm disease were a major feature of both the countryside and the suburbs. Now only a few remain, but in some places there is still plenty of shrubby hedging material left. Mature Elms make very tall and narrow, erect trees, usually with thick, deeply furrowed brown bark. Sucker growth from the base of the tree is also a major characteristic of many specimens.

Elms have a distinctive deciduous leaf when studied closely, and this differentiates them from any other species, such as *Zelkova serrata*, Japanese grey bark elm or Japanese zelkova. In all instances the two lobes of the leaf do not join the leaf stalk at the same place but are fractionally offset. Elms make flowers well before leaf break, often giving the appearance that the tree is about to break leaf, well before it is ready to do so. Few Elm bonsai are seen, and rarely is one depicted in the Japanese exhibition albums – so if a quality Elm bonsai comes your way, it is likely to be a rarity.

STYLES AND PRESENTATION

Elms are usually grown in informal, upright styles because of their erect growing habit. They are a species that cannot be made to grow contrary to their inclination. Typically they will be grown in the broom style, where all of the branches grow upright and are slightly fanned out like an upturned broom. At other times they grow in what is called a free-form upright style, with several erect growing major branches. They may also be seen in the twin-trunk style, as clumps of trees, or grown in small groups.

Trunks should always be free of blemishes unless an area has been deliberately hollowed out of a thick-trunked specimen. When in leaf the foliage should be perfect. Good

ABOVE *Ulmus elegantissima* 'Jacqueline Hillier': height 52 cm (20 in); age 7 years. Young Elms grown on rocks or in groups can make excellent bonsai.

specimens can be enjoyed in the winter for their delicate and fine ramification.

Single trees, particularly if not heavy stemmed, are often housed in long, shallow containers and planted to one end of them to enhance the stately appearance of the tree. Containers will almost invariably be glazed but not highly coloured.

SPECIES AND VARIETIES

There is no reason why any of the Elms cannot be made into bonsai. The problem is acquiring suitable material. One cultivar particularly recommended, although difficult to make into good bonsai, is the hybrid *U. elegantissima* 'Jacqueline Hillier', which has extremely small leaves and compact foliage and is easily propagated. One noted bonsai in Great Britain consists of many small specimens of the hybrid covering an impressive piece of rock. Two cultivars of *U. parvifolia*, 'Catlin' and 'Seiju', are frequently seen in American bonsai magazines.

CARE

Many of the Elms sucker freely, and when they do so on a bonsai this growth must be removed so that the sucker does not sap the tree of its strength. Some wind and sun protection in the summer is needed. In all but the small-leaved varieties the tree should be completely defoliated before midsummer, to ensure a second flush of leaves. Elms when grown as bonsai do not get attacked by Dutch elm disease.

LEFT *Ulmus procera:*
height 25 cm (10 in); age
over 30 years. Trained in the
cascade style for the last
12 years, this tree was
collected from the wild.

LEFT English or Field elm
(Ulmus procera): height
107 cm (42 in); age
30 years.

WISTERIA SPP.

DESCRIPTION

Wisteria are actually vines, not shrubs, and are commonly seen growing up the sides of walls and trailing over the top. The flowers are normally violet-blue or bluish-purple and very rarely may be pink. The flowers do not go on to make fruit of any consequence.

This is a classical flowering bonsai subject of impressive quality when well designed. Many low-quality Wisteria bonsai are imported from Japan.

BONSAI STYLES AND PRESENTATION

Wisteria do not make bonsai that conform to the standard styles; they have to be designed to show off the long racemes of flowers which can be up to 30 cm (1 ft) long. It is a species that should only be shown when in flower. Too frequently it may be found on display before the flower buds have broken. If this is the case the buds will look over-large, rather like figs, out of all proportion and most unattractive.

Very frequently Wisteria bonsai will have a trunk with a pronounced slope, through to a horizontal and maybe even a slightly cascading aspect. Pots will normally be glazed and sometimes decorated and heavy when the specimen is particularly large and cascading.

Unfortunately there are few good specimens in the West. In Japan quality Wisteria bonsai have usually been created from material collected from gardens rather than developed particularly for bonsai. When not in flower Wisteria has no interest value.

SPECIES AND VARIETIES

There are few species of this climber, and normally either Japanese wisteria (*W. floribunda*) or Chinese wisteria (*W. sinensis*) are used for bonsai. The varieties include a number of colours, from white to shades of blue, purple and pink. One cultivar of *W. floribunda*, 'Macrobotrys', has flower racemes of between 30 cm to 1.5 m (1–5 ft) in length!

CARE

Wisteria is a quick grower, needing a lot of attention to keep it under control. It tends to become top heavy with foliage after flowering and is easily blown over unless planted in a very heavy pot, or in a pot that is tied down to the staging (shelving) on which it is kept.

It is a species that most growers find difficult to make flower, either consistently or at all. Every bonsai book suggests a number of approaches to encourage flowering, but when grown from ungrafted nursery stock, the specimen will not flower, no matter what is done, unless it is of a certain age. Whatever the case, fertilizers low in nitrogen must be applied for most of the year to encourage flower bud production.

OPPOSITE Chinese wisteria *(Wisteria sinensis):* height, including pot, 36 cm (14 in); age 12 years. In training for three years, this Wisteria is grown as a cascading styled bonsai to allow the flowers to be displayed at their best.

ZELKOVA SPP.

DESCRIPTION

It is only in comparatively recent times that Zelkovas have been used for bonsai, and now small, imported Zelkovas are often available in bonsai nurseries. They are usually styled into brooms because their normal growth is like that of an upturned old fashioned besom, or broom.

Zelkovas make massive deciduous trees with powerful trunks, and with bark of an interesting quality and colour. The leaves are large, and Elm-like, and for this reason Zelkovas are often confused with Elms. However, the two lobes of the Zelkova leaf join at the same point, while on the Elm they are slightly offset. Like the Elms they have practically no leaf stalk. Autumn colour is very good, and is enhanced through the process of defoliation, making an even more fiery display of the bronze-orange and red hues that can form when autumn conditions are right.

BONSAI STYLES AND PRESENTATION

Zelkovas are usually only seen as brooms. Superior specimens are grown singly, with roots radiating evenly across the surface of the pot. The trunk is powerful and sometimes quite short, and it carries on it a very fine tracery of twigs. The stem must be perfect and without blemishes, unless the trunk has been deliberately hollowed out. Roots must be evenly spread and unobtrusive.

There are many variants to the broom. Quite likely it will be displayed when out of leaf rather than in, but when in leaf Zelkovas will usually have a solid head of foliage. Smaller-scale, single trees are often displayed in long, shallow trays, planted off-centre towards one end. Sometimes they may be in groups, and when this is the case trees of many different sizes are used to give the arrangement a feeling of considerable depth.

ABOVE *Zelkova serrata:* height 13 cm (5 in); width 20 cm (8 in); age 20 years.

Zelkova is also grown with its roots over a rock, and it is considered a suitable subject for the literati style.

Pots are usually shallow, elegant, and light in both colour and appearance. Often whites and subdued creams are used, sometimes with a light flecking of a sympathetic colour.

SPECIES AND VARIETIES

Zelkovas only have a few species, and normally the Saw-leaved or Japanese zelkova (*Z. serrata*) is used for bonsai. Varieties are few and far between.

CARE

To keep leaves small, Zelkova is usually defoliated in the year it is repotted. Defoliation is customarily done by hand stripping the leaves *en masse* rather than cutting through the many leaves with scissors. Other than that, it has no special cultivation or maintenance requirements.

ABOVE RIGHT A detail of the same Zelkova arrangement in winter clothes, and (right) in late summer.

FOLLOWING PAGE
Zelkova serrata: height 79 cm (31 in); width 97 cm (38 in); age 45 years.

APPENDIX

A GUIDE TO THE APPRECIATION OF BONSAI

Trees on public display should always be in the peak of condition, but it should be borne in mind that each can be enjoyed to their fullest at different times of the year. Unfortunately, it will not always be possible to see bonsai at their best viewing height and optimum distance when on public display due to the limitations of the display area, so due allowance should be made. The following pointers are all generalities but an understanding of them will help you to evaluate and therefore appreciate bonsai.

GENERAL POINTS

- There should be a greater depth of foliage mass behind the trunk than forward of it.

- When viewed from the side, the tree should not appear to be flattened into one plane.

- Any man-made cuts should not be visible unless created as specific features.

- The tree should not appear to lean backward. An informal-style tree should have the apex leaning forward slightly as though to greet its master.

- If the tree is still under training any wiring must be unobtrusive and certainly no bright aluminium wire should be visible. Any wire must have been applied neatly and none should appear on the trunk.

ROOTS

- Roots should run flat along the surface of the compost and not be raised out of the ground, other than in trees grown in the exposed root style.

ABOVE RIGHT *Forsythia suspensa:* height 40 cm (16 in); age 10 years. This specimen shows an inverse taper to the trunk.

BOTTOM RIGHT
Sageretia theezans: height 60 cm (24 in); age 55 years. Bonsai can be enjoyed even when out of leaf.

- Roots should radiate out evenly from around the base of the trunk.

- Major roots should be located at the sides of the trunk and not protrude directly forwards.

TRUNK

- The trunk should flare out at the base and should not descend directly into the ground like a sapling.

- The trunk should taper gently from ground level to the apex.

- The trunk should not exhibit inverse taper – that is, it should not be thinner at the base than at other points.

- Half to two-thirds of the trunk should be visible from the front in order to reveal the structure of the tree.

- The trunk should be clear of blemishes other than those specifically created for artistic effect, and these should look natural.

- Trees with any degree of slope to the trunk should start to slope from ground level.

- It should only be possible to tell grafted trees by close inspection.

RIGHT *Pinus sylvestris* 'Waterii' – a dwarf form of Scots pine; height 28 cm (11 in); age 15 years; in an unusual slanting style.

BRANCHES

- Branches should normally commence at around one-third to half of the height of the tree.

- Branches should be evenly distributed around the trunk and come off it at different levels. No two branches should normally appear at the same level.

- A higher branch should always be smaller in diameter than those lower down.

- No branch should lie directly above another in a parallel arrangement.

- No branch should cross another except in the literati style.

- There should be no unsightly bulge where the branch comes off the trunk.

- Branches should taper from the trunk through to the tip.

- The shape of the branches should all be similar and not be a mixture of straight, stiff and curved.

- No branch other than very high in the tree should point directly forward as though to poke out the eye of the viewer.

SILHOUETTE

- Depending on the species, the silhouette should either be triangular in shape, with the apex of the triangle at the top of the tree, or be gently rounded in the crown.

- Trees with multitrunks should have an overall triangular silhouette or exhibit a number of triangular outlines partially overlaying each other.

LEFT Common juniper (*Juniperus communis*) grown in the windswept style.

LEFT White or Japanese beech (*Fagus crenata*) grown as a forest planting, and excellent even without any foliage. This classical bonsai was designed by one of Japan's leading bonsai masters.

LEFT Field maple (*Acer campestre*) growing over a rock; height 33 cm (13 in); seven years in training.

- Group plantings may either have an overall triangular or rounded silhouette, or appear as a series of overlaid triangles.

- The shape of the silhouette in some groups may be disturbed by one much taller tree dominating the others.

FOLIAGE, FLOWERS AND FRUIT

- The foliage should always be in the peak of condition, looking fresh and healthy and not sickly.

- There should be no dead or diseased leaves through fungal, insect or environmental damage.

- Leaves should not show lime deposits from being misted or sprayed with hard tap water.

- No insects should be present on the tree other than a money-spider, which all respectable bonsai are likely to have.

- All leaves should be of a similar size. Any overlarge ones should be removed before display and not trimmed down to size with scissors.

- All flowers and fruit must be in peak condition showing no damage or blemishes.

POTS

- Pots should be spotlessly clean and undamaged. Brown containers may be oiled to give a sparkle to the pot.

- The colour of the pot should not clash with the dominant colour of the tree when on show, whether its foliage – spring or autumn colour – flowers or fruit.

LEFT Sloe (*Prunus spinosa*): height 23 cm (9 in); age approximately 22 years. This bonsai was collected from the wild and planted on a rock 13 years ago.

LEFT Mountain pine (*Pinus mugo*): height 26 cm (10 in); age 15 years. This pine is still under training, and needs some attention to the root formation.

LEFT *Berberis thunbergii*: height 15cm (6 in); age 10 years. This pot is a little too large to display the tree at its best.

Glazed pots are generally considered better for deciduous and broadleaved evergreen trees. Unglazed pots are generally used for coniferous evergreens.

The tree should not be planted centrally in the pot other than when a round or square one is used. The tree should be placed slightly off-centre and slightly toward the back of the pot. The precise position depends on the tree and the required illusion.

The tree should not be planted in an over-large pot: visually, it is better for a bonsai to be under-potted.

Plain pots complement more austere subjects like Black pines.

More ornate pots are more suitable for flowering and fruiting specimens or inform-ally styled trees, but should not distract attention from the tree.

COMPOST SURFACE

The surface of the compost should not be flat but raised gently toward the bole of the tree, otherwise the tree will seem sunken in the pot and make it look sad rather than bold and proud.

The surface should be free of weeds and other debris. A covering of mosses and/or gravel is preferable to an unadorned surface of prepared compost.

No dead flowers, fruit or leaves should appear on the surface of the compost, but judiciously placed flowers or fruit in peak condition may well enhance the illusion of a natural setting.

ABOVE A Chinese miniature landscape arrangement using petrified wood.

BELOW Chinese juniper;
note the drift-wood apex.

RIGHT Japanese
mountain maple *(Acer
palmatum)*: height 23 cm
(9 in); age 8 years – placed
in a *tokonoma* setting with
an accent planting of *Picea
abies* 'Nidiformis'.

- The positioning of small ceramic or wooden animals and other objects on the surface of the compost is a Chinese practice, and not really to Western taste unless applied with considerable discrimination.

MULTITRUNKED BONSAI

- Multitrunked trees should have all stems rising from ground level, and not from part way up the trunk.

- All stems should emerge close together, gradually diverging as they ascend, and looking as though they are all part of the same entity.

- All stems should be the same general shape and gently curved, not stiff.

- The thickness of an individual trunk should be in proportion to its height.

MULTITREE PLANTINGS

- All trunks should be visible when viewed from the front and from the side.

- The tallest and therefore dominant tree should be raised at ground level above the others.

- Space should be left in the pot to imply a natural expanse of open ground.

- The thicknesses of individual trunks should be in proportion to their heights.

CASCADES

- There may be a number of cascading tails, none of which should touch the rim of the pot.

- Cascades do not necessarily have to have a head of foliage above the cascading tail, but when they do, the general line of the sweep of the trunk and head of foliage should be in the direction of the tail.

- The tail should come off the trunk at an angle rather than appearing to have been artificially bent over.

- The tip of the tail should not be on the same level as the base of the pot.

- Pots should be much deeper than normally used for bonsai, and are specially made for this style of tree.

- Cascade bonsai should be displayed on a stand that is a different height to that of the pot.

GLOSSARY

Apex The highest point of a tree, whether it be living or dead, in the form of a *jin*; as in the case of a cascade it could be part of the trunk.

Bonkei A tray landscape representing a natural scene which will contain rocks and low-growing plants as well as trees.

Bonsai A tree (or shrub or vine) growing in an appropriate and decorative container, but styled in an artistic manner representing a version in miniature of a real-life tree.

Buttressing The flaring out at the base of a tree which takes place as a tree moves from sapling stage to one that has a feeling of age and stability.

Classical bonsai Those species that are traditionally used for bonsai or that make outstanding trees (eg Pine, Maple, Juniper, Spruce).

Cossetting Taking special care of a tree in winter by protecting it against the cold.

Cultivar A plant variety produced from a naturally occurring species that is maintained by cultivation.

Deciduous A plant that sheds its leaves in the autumn each year.

Defoliation The complete removal of all the leaves of a deciduous tree to help reduce its leaf size and improve autumn colour.

Evergreen A plant that remains in leaf the whole of the year. Leaves are either shed annually over a period of time or remain for a few years before being replaced.

Genus A grouping of plants that have similar, distinguishing characteristics; the main subdivision of a family of plants. A genus may contain one or more species and if it does it is followed by the abbreviation spp. (ie *Quercus* spp.)

Indoor bonsai Species that need to be kept indoors for the majority of the year, although they usually appreciate being outside during the summer. They are more difficult to maintain than ordinary bonsai.

Jin An artificial deadwood effect on a bonsai in the form of a vestigial stub, either at the apex or on the trunk where a branch once was.

Literati style A style of bonsai that complies to no set rules as do most other bonsai styles. Literati trees have thin trunks and are spartan of foliage, which is usually confined to the upper reaches of the tree.

Mame The name given to small-scale bonsai, usually less than 15 cm (6 in) in height including the pot – pronounced marmay.

Ramification The division of branches into sub-branches and finally to twiglets.

Re-acclimatization Getting used to new conditions, particularly when the change from one set of conditions to another would be severe – such as from the hot and dry atmosphere of a centrally heated room to ice cold conditions outdoors.

Repotting A necessary procedure undertaken to stimulate the vigour of a tree. For some specimens it may be done yearly, for others as infrequently as every 10 years.

Rosette In the form of a rose.

Seasonal bonsai Species that are only at their best for a short and specific time of the year.

Suiban A shallow tray with no drainage holes often filled with gravel or water, to house a bonsai on a rock.

Species A distinct kind of plant having certain, distinguishing characteristics; the subdivision under genus. A species may or may not contain varieties.

Tokonoma A display area in a Japanese house in the form of an alcove where a bonsai is placed, together with an accent planting and a scroll.

Tree Most bonsai growers refer to their bonsai as trees rather than referring to them as bonsai, and in this work the use of the word tree is usually synonymous with the word bonsai.

Variety A distinct group of plants having specific features of its own within a species.

ABOVE *Juniperus squamata* 'Meyeri': height 132 cm (52 in); ages 4 to 20 years. Grown from nursery stock and formed as a small group planting, the trees show dead-wood effects.

INDEX

ACKNOWLEDGEMENTS

Key: *t* = top; *b* = bottom; *l* = left; *r* = right; *c* = centre.

Dan Barton: pages 14, 20 *b,* 29, 31, 32, 35, 45 *b,* 52, 57 *b,* 63, 67, 81, 90, 91, 99, 105, 104, 115, 121 *t b c,* 122 *t.*
Photos Larry Bray (bonsai owned by Peter Chan): pages 10, 21, 24, 30, 37 *l r,* 36, 42, 41, 51 *l,* 54, 57 *t,* 58 *b,* 61, 62 *t,* 97.
Photos courtesy of the Federation of British Bonsai Societies (of Bonsai shown at their exhibition at Nottingham in 1985): pages 64 (**Mark R Abbot, Manchester**); 25, 76 *t l* (**Peter M Brown**); 12 *t,* 60 *t* (**grower; Peter Chan**); 111 (**D E J Claridge**); 51 *r,* 125 **Craig Coussins, Scotland**); 15 (*mame* selection by **Mrs Ivy Murray**); 20 *t;* 47, 72 *b,* 76 *r,* 89 (**Harry Tomlinson**).
Photos Paul Forrester (bonsai owned by Gordon Owen): pages 16, 19, 23, 33, 39, 62 *b,* 87, 107, 106, 108, 110.
Photos by and bonsai owned by Paul Goff: pages 11 *b,* 7 *t,* 22, 26, 56, 59, 60 *b,* 74, 80 *t,* 113, 120, 122 *c b,* 124 *l r,* front and back jacket.
Photos by and bonsai owned by Bill Jordan: pages 43, 65, 92, 96, 116, 117 *t b,* 118.
Colin Lewis: pages 13 *b,* 45 *t,* 44, 66, 72 *t,* 73, 95, 112.
Gordon Owen: pages 7 *b,* 12 *b,* 13 *t,* 11 *t,* 76 *bl,* 80 *b,* 84.
© **Wan Li Book Company Ltd:** pages 6, 8, 27, 28, 48, 49, 53, 55, 58 *t,* 68, 69, 71, 75, 77, 79, 83 *t b,* 85, 93, 94, 101, 103, 119 *t b,* 123.